Willingness:
A Writer's Meditations on Crossing the Flood

Willingness:
A Writer's Meditations on Crossing the Flood

Kevin "Mc" McIlvoy
with
Christine Hale

wtaw press
Santa Rosa, CA

Introduction by Peter Turchi
Edited by Peg Alford Pursell
Cover art: Kevin McIlvoy

Library of Congress Cataloging-in-Publication data
is on file with the Library of Congress.

ISBN: 979-8-9898729-7-8 (paperback)
ISBN: 979-8-9898729-8-5 (ebook)

WTAW Press
PO Box 2825
Santa Rosa, CA 95405
www.wtawpress.org

WTAW Press is a not-for-profit literary press. This publication is made possible by the generous contributions from individual donors, public arts organizations, and private foundations.

For everyone who loved Mc, and learned from him.

How, dear sir, did you cross the flood?

By not halting, friend, and by not straining I crossed the flood. When I came to a standstill, friend, then I sank; but when I struggled, then I got swept away. It is in this way, friend, that by not halting and by not straining I crossed the flood.

(*The Connected Discourses of the Buddha*,
a translation of the *Samyattu Nikāya* by Bikkhu Bodhi)

Contents

In 152 words:
everything Mc McIlvoy ever taught

Honoring the will of the work to impart, enact.
Honoring the will of the work to enact, impart.

Holding to fluid understanding of unity, unify.
Holding to fluid understanding of instability, destabilize.

Inviting overwhelming engagement, estrange.
Inviting overwhelming estrangement, engage.

Acknowledging the gifts of co-consciousness,
sustain the silences.
Acknowledging the gifts of subconscious processes,
crowd the darknesses.

Nesting order inside chaos, sensitize language's body.
Nesting chaos inside order, excite language's body.

Witnessing the drama of present experience
perishing, regard the enigmas of eternity.
Witnessing the ineffable in the experience of time
and space, evoke presence mindfully.

Experiencing prehensive solitary rapture,
the reader feels the full scale of self-love.
Experiencing prehensive communal horror,
the reader feels the full scale of love for humanity.

In waves, the artist's love uncovers the greater loves.
In waves, the greater loves uncover the artist's loves.

What is before us is enough.*
What is before us is enough.

*Bashō

Foreword

Mc composed the foregoing set of koans in 2005. For some of his students, friends, and readers, those succinct instructions will be *enough*. But for many, including me, some unpacking may be helpful.

At the time of his sudden death in September 2022, Mc was in discussions with WTAW Press publisher Peg Alford Pursell about a nonfiction book, to be entitled *Willingness,* on his methods of teaching the craft of writing and of instigating creative process. She, along with many of his former students, wished to ensure a lasting record of his unique ways of investigating, encouraging, and responding to the art of storytelling.

During the summer of 2022 as he worked on the book, he sometimes talked to me about it. He told me that he wanted the book to be about his "process of searching" as writer, teacher, and editor. He invoked as a kind of model Italo Calvino's *Six Memos for the New Millennium* (also unfinished due to that writer's death; the book, despite its title, includes just five memos) and emphasized that he wished *not* to offer prescriptive advice on how to write but rather to spur artistic introspection and exploration of craft among fellow seekers. When Mc left us, he left behind this book's title and subtitle—*Willingness: A Writer's Meditations on Crossing the Flood;* the epigraph from which the subtitle is derived; and some finished sections, including The Overplus, The Writer's Act of Faith, and The Fatal Gaze.

In compiling and editing this book, I've sought to rigorously honor the intent he described to me. What he had completed, I've retained. The rest of the material I've excerpted and collaged, drawing from his lectures, class notes and handouts, published and unpublished essays, recent published interviews, and in a few cases where I hadn't yet found his language for key concepts, emails and handwritten notes. I chose to use the koans of "152 Words..." to structure the book because they invite the associative, recursive, branching-rather-than-arriving experience of listening to and learning from Mc. Beyond this foreword, the words are his and their arrangement mine. Subheads are as much as possible Mc's words, sometimes lifted from his "lecture ladders" (these are included among the "Extras" at the back of the book). For readability throughout *Willingness*, I've eschewed the use of brackets and ellipses, and relied on my familiarity with him and his ways to guard against misrepresenting him as I edited.

Mc deeply appreciated and was driven creatively by paradox. He was endlessly, exuberantly performative. He exalted compression and ellipsis. He was, as he once wrote of Thoreau, "literate in approximately twelve million kinds of silence." He taught by indirection, suggestion, and provocation. Readers and students often described his fiction and his methods as "wild"—which might be a testament to how fully he realized his aspiration to "radically decenter" them—but he underpinned everything he wrote and taught with structure. He had a well-defined philosophy of learning and, as the epigraph he chose for this book implies, an indefatigable *willingness* to be open to the question and—in response to it—"the better question."

Great literature, he believed, arose from "the dynamic convergence of the author's will, the will of the work itself, and the will of the reader." In nearly a half-century of service to that passionate conviction—as writer, teacher, mentor, and editor—he strove to help writers "unlearn hardened assumptions about the reader, to liberate writers to be at play inside the work, and to guide them in discerning surprising possibilities in which the work presents its own terms of engagement in dynamic opposition to the author's design intentions." To that end, he taught "the risk-taking processes through which we learn the habits of presence" and "concepts that challenge the writer's first assumptions about the will of the work, the will of the writer, and the will of the reader," including "enacting and imparting, grounded and ungrounded experience, resistance and receptivity, somatic aliveness, co-consciousness, nonutilitarian delight, trust in prehension and not exclusively in comprehension," all in service "of unlearning willfulness, of learning willingness." (I've quoted here from Mc's "The Terms of Engagement Between Author and Editor" and his "Teaching Philosophy," included in this book's "Extras.")

On paper and in person, Mc could be by turns fierce, funny, tender, admonitory, irreverent, didactic, subversive. His opinions, as more than one long-time friend has said, were "intense," yet he was also an openhearted person and an extraordinary listener. Joe Scapellato, a self-described "technically former (but truly continual) student" of Mc's, wrote in his editor's note to the publication of Mc's story "Tartarus" in the journal *West Branch*, "There are things Mc said to me, years ago, and ways in which Mc listened to the things that other people said to him, years ago, that continue to root and bloom in me.... He was The Example of how to be the very best kind of forever-student."

To be always a learner-teacher was an enduring ambition for Mc. He said of himself, in a first-day-of-class lecture delivered somewhere in his nearly thirty years as professor at New Mexico State University:

> I don't know—in the larger sense—what is required of us as learners and by what path we will determine and achieve those requirements. I *don't know.*
>
> With you I will learn how to sail past established routes, the known world of thought and expression in order to make a long journey to the mother of the mother of the mother of all our accepted assumptions.

He aspired, as well, to write and to teach as expression of his spiritual practice. To that end, he cultivated in himself and others an openness, a "stance of wonder" (John Berryman), toward creative process. He spoke of this in a talk to the North Carolina Writers Network in November 2019:

> And what is this humble practice you are engaged in—a practice that for 99.9 percent of us will not likely ever bring power or wealth?
>
> What is the practice of gazing—and gazing—and more deeply gazing—and losing ourselves in the gazing—and seeing what is before us as never before—and *becoming* what is before us—and gazing—and seeing ourselves from within the thing or person that storytelling has allowed us to *become*?
>
> What is this practice? Here's what I believe:

> It is the truest practice of selfless, pleasurable, pleasurably difficult *compassion.*
>
> May this compassion always inform our writing—may it deepen with each story we write—may it begin after we have finished writing today and before we begin writing tomorrow.

On that note—in that stance—let us enter the flood of *Willingness.*

Christine Hale

Introduction

This book is a gift.

Willingness: A Writer's Meditations on Crossing the Flood offers insights on writing (and reading, and being) by short story writer, novelist, poet, editor, and veteran teacher Kevin ("Mc," he would insist) McIlvoy. To those of us who knew him—taught with him, studied with him—he was legendary. One reason: he had an original voice, an original vision, a way of seeing both writing and the world not quite like anyone else's, as the pages that follow illustrate.

Another: his readings and lectures often began with silence. Mc would approach the podium, pause, draw from his right rear pocket the printed pages of his text—which he had folded, then folded again—unfold them, and then look out at the audience, often for an uncomfortable length of time. Long enough for some in the audience to laugh, in awkward anticipation. Mc would confess to being nervous in front of audiences, but he was in performative mode. He fully inhabited his readings, singing as much as speaking. His lectures were usually accompanied by perplexing handouts of his own devising: lecture ladders, a few samples of which are included here. If you read one of those ladders and think, But what exactly was that lecture about? you have joined the crowd. Mc was in many ways playful—as playful as he was serious. The ladder would take on meaning, coherence, only in the context of the lecture. Until then, it was an object of wonder, open to the reader's interrogation.

A third reason for his legendariness: Mc was, as a reader and fellow-writer, famously generous. He not only read the work of his friends and former students, but wrote to them about it, often in great detail. He was open to, and encouraged, all sorts of work, from the seemingly conventional to the highly experimental; he received it as it was offered.

A fourth: Mc was an other-worldly DJ. He read the dance floor every bit as sensitively as he read Stephen Crane or Anaïs Nin. ("Do you know what they want next?" he would say to me over the roar of the music. "They want Prince. They don't know it yet, but they want Prince.")

If you were one of the many fortunate to interact with Mc over the decades of his career, you'll recognize, with pleasure, what he and Chris Hale have provided us here: excerpts from his lectures and interviews, those lecture ladders, exercises, and his near-mythic instructions for "voice collecting." Reading through this collection, I was particularly delighted to see excerpts from the first class of his I remember hearing (on silences; I vividly recall thinking, as I entered the room, How will he possibly talk about this for seventy-five minutes? and thinking, as I left the room, He could have gone on for three hours.), as well as from his lectures on imminence, and useless beauty, and sex scenes. As demonstrated here, Mc had no hesitation to mix the sacred and the profane, a discussion of God and a call for more good sex. "I find it is consoling to hear the 'take' of James Brown's 'Love Don't Love Nobody' on the reissue of Messing with the Blues," he says here,

> in which the finished song and the take have been published together. On the take, about twenty-five seconds in, Brown stops his amazing tailpipe-dragging-sparks-flying singing because the sound engineer breaks in to convey a message from someone—I'm pretty sure it is God—saying, "That was a good start, man—make it more of a melodic thing—you sang the hell out it—but just a little more melody."

By now it should be obvious that, whatever this is, it isn't a craft book—by which I mean, one of those well-intentioned books meaning to instruct its readers on the fundamental elements of character development, scene, plot, etc. And yet it is a craft book, in the much larger sense of a book that means to converse with fellow artists about making art. In these pages, Mc offers instruction about very little, suggestions about virtually everything. As often as he offers advice in these pages, Mc poses questions.

This book welcomes us. It also resists us—resists our typical reading, if our typical reading is to move paragraph to paragraph, page to page, at a steady pace, with an eye toward gathering what we can as we move ahead efficiently, to get to the end, to get to the point where we can say, "I've read this book *Willingness*," implying, "I've finished it. Bring on the next book." This is a book to spend time with, to contemplate. To return to.

Several things will become evident to any reader of this book, whatever their previous knowledge of the author. Mc had a high tolerance for—some might say addiction to—doubled phrases ("Was that choice you made a 'workmanship of risk' choice—or a 'workmanship of certainty' choice"; "the editor assists the author in processes of revision that are, after all, processes of unlearning willfulness, or learning willingness") and reversed phrasing ("An old voice has more moments of emptiness that are full; it has more moments of fullness struck through with emptiness"; "the drama of sound-thinking, the drama of think-sounding"). As Chris suggests in her Foreword, these are a reflection of Mc's long interest in koans. It will soon become clear that Mc prized mystery (not obscurity) and risk: "In all phases of writing and research I give high priority to the discovery of…transformative strangeness," he tells us, and "paradox is the essence of really rich art," and "We should not write The Teachable. And we should revise in such a way that we scrutinize the value of The Teachable." Again and again he talks about defamiliarization, destabilization, putting aside our desire to impose our will on the work and, instead, listening to the will of the work.

Mc was, throughout his long career, particularly attentive to voice. This is no surprise to anyone familiar with his collections *Singing Lessons*, or *57 Octaves Below Middle C*, or who heard him perform one of his pieces composed entirely of infield chatter. His attention to how we communicate with one another—and fail to—transcended any common advice about the presentation of dialogue. "I've always trusted incoherence above coherence," he says here; and "You could say that you had been present for singing and that the singing had been so spellbinding that almost from the first words you gave up any expectation of directionality of narrative"; and "I place my first trust as storyteller in the human voice."

This book is a gift. I look forward to sharing it with others. But—and I feel certain Mc would agree—we should not merely accept this gift, as if it were a comfortable sweater, or a beloved cousin's inedible biscuits. We should argue with it, find fault in it, talk back to it; we should adjust it to fit; we should value its mysteries as much as its mastery; we should recognize it as an act of devotion, shared with us.

Peter Turchi

Mc on Mc—

Artist's Statement (May 2020)

In creating art I eagerly anticipate "radical decentering." This term, used by the philosopher Elaine Scarry (in her astonishing masterpiece *On Beauty & Being Just*), describes how our simplest and most complex encounters with dark and luminous beauty remove from us our assumption that we exist in a centered condition, remove from us our very assumption that we should wish for such certainty, for such invulnerability. Artists trust vulnerability and uncertainty, and we trust the sense that every manifestation of beauty before us asks us to become it. Since twenty-first century American culture values the controlling, tough, self-centered ideas of capitalism above the relenting, tender, self-forgetting ideals of democracy, life for American artists is brutal. Brutal and, often, brief.

As one who has presumed (for almost forty years!) to teach artists, I have observed that the artists who burn out first are the ones who repeatedly seek safety and predictability in their habits of construction and creativity; I have observed that the artists who burn intensely and keep burning and keep burning are the ones whose habits of construction and creativity welcome radical decentering.

Crossing the Flood...

Honoring the will of the work to impart, enact.

Honoring the will of the work to enact, impart.

In writing my novels and short stories, I try to value felt experience above thought experience. My novels and short stories are my practice in sustaining a Zen initiate's form of "beginner's mind," and they inform my teaching both in the ways they fail and in the ways they succeed.

When I have presumed to teach writing, I've tried to say to writers, "Make sure that it is pleasurable and satisfying to you to write. That will mean you will need to be in the process of self-examination in which you say, 'To what degree am I turning away from all the first principles that have been the pillars of my belief system as a human being and as an artist?'"

Jeopardize the agenda

I am a learner. I ask other learners to join me in placing their minds and hearts at risk inside and outside the classroom.

I am a believer in the Socratic method in which each member of a community of learners agrees to upset the agendas, perspective, and sensibilities of everyone else in the community of learners. I offer what I can, already knowing that the processes through which you will dispute, transform, or systematically dismiss what I say are all that matters.

Learning by the agenda is a well-defined, reward-based, product-oriented form of learning uncomplicated by recognition of multiple truths or by regard for individual definitions of integrity.

We do not have to put aside the agenda all at once in order to develop further as learners—a convention of anarchists is never a true community of learners—but we certainly have to constantly jeopardize the agenda.

One way we can do that is by having a personal learning philosophy to live with and by—one preferably that you live uneasily with or by, so that it serves as a tension inside you that will not give your heart or mind rest.

Here's one that makes me uneasy because I believe it is true even when sometimes I wish it were not: Engagement *and* Estrangement Are Both Good Teachers. Freud's and Jung's methodologies were appalling yet their assertions were so seductively engaging they altered history. How? They were endlessly arguable, endlessly questionable, and the processes of argument and questioning they set in motion have clearly superseded in importance the original assertions.

And here's one that every good elementary teacher must believe who crowds the classroom with world globes and maps and giant alphabet letters and bells and prisms and odd smells: To Encourage Creativity, Invite Distraction. When our minds are *journeying* they are active.

I believe in the risk of having a personal learning philosophy like the one reflected in William Butler Yeats' dictum: "passionate impulse and patient pains are not incompatible." It complicates all my notions of desire and ambition. To live at risk as learners, we should have disturbing, confounding philosophies and we should impose them on the community of learners around us. This agitation offers an education that values questioning above answering.

It seems apparent that Einstein delighted less in the answers provided by his theory of relativity than in the thousand new questions it produced. Socrates did not argue for a learning system of answers; he insisted on a dialogue of questions escalating in complexity. Do not begin by unhesitatingly accepting the apparent answers provided by the forms of evidence before you but by asking, "Are we proposing the right *questions* about this body of evidence?" A good question responded to not by an answer but by a better question invites imagination, which is the transformer of perspective.

Some of the most successful journeys of thought begin in absurdly small boats in which we are vulnerable and cannot depend on what we have learned in safer, larger, more conventional crafts. When our processes of questioning *defamiliarize* what seems familiar to us, we can form new premises.

The learner whose entire formative education has been conventionally agenda-driven will resist these forms of questioning and will say we are merely avoiding answering. And it is true that when we are questioners, as children are questioners, we practice a kind of innocence that is startling. We practice a kind of unselfconscious truthsearching that values the indefinable as much as the definite.

Respond to the dark and luminous body of the work

Broadly, my philosophy of writing the novel is that sentence by sentence, you let everything in. You picture yourself as a person in a very small untrustworthy boat way out in the middle of the ocean with a giant net, and every pull you make to bring it in, whatever you've caught, threatens to capsize you, but everything in that net belongs there. Then, at a certain stage, sentence by sentence, you start to say, "Maybe not this one, maybe not that one."

As a fiction writer, when I'm writing I am not practicing the control of language; I am with language learning what it brings, by which

I mean I am practicing dynamic balance of intuitive and conscious artistry. I am aware that a world is made through the alteration of a word. If I write, "A small lamp was somewhere on his desk," I have described a completely different consciousness than, "A small lamp was on his desk."

In my process of composing, I work really slowly on the first fifty to one hundred words; I'm exploring the root notes of voice; the sense of space and time; the affective, organic structure. Not the effective machinery of the structure of ordering and meaning-making but the affective structure of pulse, flow, and the pressures of silences and absences. In crafting, I'm not trying to find the *direction* of the work. I'm wishing to feel my whole body responding to the *ground* of the work.

Once these fifty to one hundred words have given me some sense of what the work itself wishes to be—once the will of the work has significantly obliterated my own willfulness—then I feel I have the willingness to put down a chaotic, all-but-unreadable whole draft (of a novel or novella chapter, of a short story, a prose poem, etc.).

Both of these stages of composing are slow, slow stages of pleasure-making and pleasure-taking for me.

Revision in the first stages is, for me, a commitment to learn from my time on the rough draft (for some reason, I always find myself accidentally darkening that word to "raft"), what the essential wild nature of the work asks me to *feel*—I didn't say *know* because I trust most the knowing that naturally results from fullness of feeling as opposed to the knowing that merely generates more knowing.

Revision in the next stages is a commitment to the slow, slow, pleasure-making and pleasure-taking of learning authorial generosity. The artist who hurries revision learns efficiency. The artist unhurriedly responding to the terrifyingly luminous and luxuriously dark body of the work learns generosity.

Because revision for me takes far longer than composing, it humbles me more profoundly and alters me more permanently—in the big picture of my life as an artist—than composing.

If I intuitively feel—*feel*-know, not know-feel—that dynamic opposing forces give the draft page fullness—forces of silence and singing, of articulation and expressive inarticulateness, of spilling and pouring—I will be happy it has grown in my garden—grown there, perhaps in spite of me—and I will continue to care for it, protect it, and learn from it how it wishes to change the whole ecology of me.

With both long and short pieces, ten to twelve comprehensive revisions is typical. I am very definitely still learning when to stop revising. In late and early stages of revision, I show drafts to readers who are both resistant and receptive to my work.

I send work out when I feel confident it represents the sum of my skills at that moment in my life. I forgive myself for the skills I'm still awkwardly developing, and I set out to learn new ways to awkwardly develop.

I keep a writing journal. At some point—usually when a new project is substantially underway and other projects are finished and are trying to find a publisher—I write journal entries about where I find myself in my process of learning to compose and revise. This kind of journal self-assessment gives me pleasure, and it re-energizes me.

Engine & enigma, testers & questers

I feel that we have been extensively, exhaustively "taught to the test," which I feel mis-measures our knowledge and which fails to measure our capacity for wisdom, which asks us to consider the beauty of the prime number, the cell, the word, and to ask only, "What use will I make of this beauty," not, "How will this beauty radically decenter me" (Elaine Scarry), place me in a condition in which I fully welcome both the concept of "use" and of "nonutilitarian delight" (Vladmir Nabokov)?

I feel that we have learned particularly well the transactional powers of language. I feel that we must learn far more about those endless powers. I worry that in the process of concentrating exclusively on that transactional power we have unlearned the transformational capacities of language.

I feel you believe that I, when nominally your "teacher," should not be a fellow learner, not be someone who feels before he thinks, who senses before he says. I feel how everyone—I include myself—is uncomfortable thinking of me as an erotic learner as often as I am an aesthetic learner. I feel you wish for me to stand apart from learning, to sustain the illusion of completeness, and not to embrace learning so tightly that I can perceive only elements of it with clarity and can feel intimately both my harmony and my disharmony with what I am embracing.

I feel that you look at me as a model of engine, a force that will drive us forward toward meaning and definition, the goals of testers.

I intend to be our model of enigma, to place us—all of us—in the stance of wonder in which we will pursue the goals of questers.

We will possess knowledge. We will be possessed by wisdom, this practice of presence into the world.

Mysteries beyond mastery

Walter Benjamin, in *Illuminations*, makes a helpful distinction between knowledge and wisdom. He writes—this is my own attempt to both distill it and feel it—that in all cultures a certain kind of story repeats itself: someone leaves her village to pursue information that might be helpful to all, present and future. When the person returns with the information, she can share it efficiently and systematically with the people of the village. This prodigal figure can exclusively bring back information—here is exactly how we should prune our trees to have them bear more fruit; this is precisely how to make a thing called a sock—or she can share both the information and her *feeling* about the information.

The first choice is loyal to *knowledge*; the second, to *wisdom*. The first will have, at last, only *use* in the village and, so, will teach mastery; the second will increase both mastery and mystery and, so, give the people in the village "power over" *and* "power to."

Our era (the era of preemptivity) has taught us well to preempt feeling and thought, to condemn any condition that is not a reflection of national conformity. This has undermined our own trust in dynamic internal conflict; it has taught us to condemn impassioned public debate by respectful opponents who might have trusted that, by its very nature, debate moves us past *imparted* knowledge into *enacted* wisdom.

We have been taught long and thoughtful silences and the simple honest and powerfully innocent statements of ignorance are unacceptable. We are supposed to know—now. Evidence of conflicting thought and feeling, of humble processes of abandoning old thought and welcoming new thought and feeling will be received impatiently.

We might come to feel that silence gives little indication of knowledge.

It might be that silence is the very essence of wisdom.

Silence is, after all, an essential part of our sound-thinking and our think-sounding. It creates in us both excited and fearful anticipation. In one of the Sibley's guides to songbirds, I remember reading this simple sentence about hawks: "When they are not screaming, they are mostly silent."

The reader brought alive

At this coming-to-an-end time, we need more than ever what Henry David Thoreau called a "realometer," a built-in sense that every positive and negative construction we perceive as "real" is elusively real and only elusively understandable. Those of us who write poems and stories are consequentialists, aren't we? In our poems and stories the more we individually dedicate ourselves to attentiveness, to full presence to the ways of being and becoming in the smallest phenomena before us, the more we recognize that the consequence will be responsiveness. When we are truly responsive, we are fully alive. Aliveness is the mission of the artist whose most powerful work causes silence, what W.B. Yeats called the moment when we live with a "clear, perhaps even with a fiercer life, because of our quiet."

A reader brought alive falls silent, and finds their authentic voice rising out of that silence. A reader brought alive is inherently radicalized.

And didn't you and I, after all, choose to write novels because as novel readers we felt invited to dare inhabit paradox more fully in our so-called "real" lives?

A novel is the embodiment of paradox. When you are living inside a novel, whatever is happening to the characters, whatever you are experiencing, is a constant invitation to come to terms with what is paradoxical.

Novels help people acknowledge the paradoxes of our world as transitive and immanent; "transitive" because we acknowledge there the contradictory ways that we are modified by what we encounter; "immanent" because we acknowledge there the contradictory ways we are always perfecting our own ways of being.

Artists commit ourselves to exploring the dark and luminous beauty that is before us; we avoid assuming that what is pretty is ever truly beautiful. I believe that no matter the nature of our projects, we discern that the question, "Is this engaging?" is not enough. At all points we must also ask, "Is this estranging?" If we do not welcome both questions, we will make art that presents completeness, an engine operating exactly as we expect; if we do not welcome the two questions, our art will not present fullness, the fullness of enigma existing beyond our complete understanding while acting upon us with what Linda Gregerson has called "repeatable surprise."

Enigma *is* the engine of the novel.

What we do is handwork

We make the clean, simple elements and the infinitely complex elements of our poetry and fiction with our hands. We are the kinds of carpenters who have not just bought so many board feet for the project; we have cut the trunks and limbs of the trees, paying close attention to the weakest and the strongest points of branching, bracing, and load-bearing. Writers are the rarest kind of architects, who must know how to harvest timber, manufacture other building materials—concrete, glass, roof shingle, floor tile, all of it—writers must know how to pour a foundation, to frame up and finish, to install the electrical, the plumbing, the heating-cooling system—and we must know how to do this in a flood plain, often in a frozen place or place of drought, often in a milieu that aggressively resists us because it wants us to reduce the quality and increase the quantity of this work we make *with our hands.*

Sometimes you hear a writer say—sadly, so sadly—"I'm starting my next book—my second book, my seventeenth book. And it feels like I've never written a book ever—a poem, a paragraph of prose, like I've never written anything resembling a sentence." When you hear this aren't you a little happy to know that the writer's habits of work and craft have made them less certain, more at risk, and, so, more free than they were one book ago or sixteen books ago?

There's benefit in being a writer with a five-decade checkered history of "successes" and "failures": the perceived failures in the work have often actually been the greatest personal successes; the perceived successes, the greatest personal failures.

Holding to fluid understanding of unity, unify.

Holding to fluid understanding of instability, destabilize.

I watched a really large wasp fly into a really small spider's flimsy made-for-flies-and-gnats web—this was in my writing studio—during time I had set aside for writing. The wasp would have escaped pretty fast but the spider hurriedly added webbing to the area near the wasp's wingtips, and it hurriedly tore down and re-rigged other parts of the web structure, and it meticulously firmed up the little bit of webbing limiting the movement of the wasp's head, and it very slowly crawled into the basement of the web in order to wrap webbing around the tip of each wasp leg. At all points in this pleasurable working and crafting, the spider, about one-twentieth the size of the wasp, paused, started again, stepped back, started again, paused. I could hear it say to the wasp, "Staying long? Of course you are...of course you are." It was harder to make out what the wasp was saying on this particular occasion of the end of its life.

Looking at that web transformed by the occasion, you could not help thinking, Beautiful—beautiful—horrifyingly beautiful—a holy web—obscene—beautiful. If you are the wasp, you can't help thinking it. Part of the web is perfectly crafted and part is hurriedly and imperfectly worked, but I don't believe its so-called "finished" beauty would be improved by removing the hurriedly made workmanlike part. Yes, it was hurriedly made, that part that trapped the prisoner's wings and its head. Still, that part—what the masters of craft call "sloppy craft"—needs to stay because without it, the meaning of the web might be apparent but not the moment of the web.

Pattern-recognizing, -disrupting, -obscuring

Fifty years into my life as an artist, I'm still learning how to look. I trust that in this journey I am putting aside the need to assert completeness in judgments and generalizations that will keep me—and, by implication, the reader—grounded in certainties. I trust that in this journey I am relenting to destabilizing questions that deepen the fullness of my compassion and connection, and that invite the reader to do the same.

The first lesson, it seems, is to recognize pattern; and the next lesson is to recognize the randomness in all so-called patterns; and the next progression of learning is to acknowledge fully the causes of dynamic randomness and its outcomes. What appears "perfect" is, by its nature, "imperfect." For some of us this is the source of our great pleasure in composing and revising. For some of us it is the heart of our grief.

Whenever I reread David Pye's book *The Nature and Art of Workmanship,* it increases my neurotic pleasure, my pleasurable neurosis. He writes, "In the workmanship of risk rough work is the necessary basis of the perfect work, just as the sketch is of the picture...the first approximations of the workman may afterwards disappear as the work proceeds, or they may be left standing....In the workmanship of certainty there is no rough work." Needless to say, he's not encouraging carelessness or ineptitude; he is calling for what he calls "free workmanship," the process in which there is as much evidence of relenting control as of controlling.

Concision and precision are values we learned as essay writers in our business-model American early education. More often than not, the novel's asymmetrical and excessive materials reflect the virtues of concision and precision only in order to undo the business they seem to serve. Reread passages from your favorite novels, and you will be reminded that novelistic sentences (including sentences occurring in scene and dialogue treatment) are not at all models of effective transaction but of affective transformation.

In revising the early whole drafts of your novel, I ask that you consider finding your own structured manner of assessing the inherent values in the rough pages. I ask that you postpone confronting your novel's great number of flaws until you can consider all flaws, large and small, only in light of the will of the work.

I do not ask you to ignore the flaws. I ask that you come to them next.

Hiding the wolves, hiding from them

A person who wants that unique sound of John Lee Hooker on a song like "The Waterfront" or "Stop Now Baby" will want a guitar that in open tuning has a crunch-huh-howl whenever the F# is fingered on any fret. That flawed wonder is called the "wolf tone," and it is characteristic of other kinds of stringed instruments. Some cellists choose to correct it with a "wolf tone eliminator" or "wolf suppressor" placed between the bridge and the tailpiece. These eliminators and suppressors come in various sizes suited to the sonic qualities of individual instruments. Other cellists choose to minimize but not eliminate the wolf tone, since, after all, it is almost impossible. The instrument maker Chris Dungey writes that "every properly proportioned cello has a wolf tone," and the restorer Ken Meyer says, "the better the instrument is adjusted, the worse the wolf shows. When the instrument is not well adjusted, all the pitches are wobbling. There's no ring while you play and the harmonics are off pitch. This can hide the wolves or make for just general wolfy areas."

The effect of the imperfect instrument is that the performer, neither wishing to "hide the wolves" nor to place the music in the "general wolfy areas" must adjust technique. The moments of equilibrium in the music are not undone by the artist's pact with the wolves; the moments of dynamic balance are not lost as a result of the artist either hiding the wolves or hiding from them. For those of us wishing to make distinctions between work that we might name as "unconventional" and work we might name as "experimental," it is worth considering the degree to which the artist has altered the instruments toward dynamic balance and away from equilibrium.

I use the term "equilibrium" to describe the effect of elements of substance and style completing or cancelling each other out in a way that invites recognition of pattern and of patterned balance. I use the term "dynamic balance" to describe the effect of work that in substance and style is, at the very same moment, on the verge of falling into and falling out of balance, and that invites acknowledgement of quasi-pattern and quasi-balance.

Consider two terms from acoustic engineering: directionality (the listener knows where the sound originates, how to find it, how to follow it where it leads) and surroundability (the listener's inability to identify the sound's direction, the listener's uncanny sense that it is coming from both outside and inside us). The reader wishing for the work to be perfect in its design does not quite welcome passages evoking surroundability, which interfere with the forward progression of the various plot elements and ask the reader to be inside daydreams or reveries. These wolves balance and unbalance the work at the same moment. The reader does not welcome them, but, feeling their rightness, moves back and forth from a state of equilibrium to a state of dynamic balance during the reading experience.

Immediately upon completing the whole first draft, novelists who are, by nature, over-humble and over-proud, resolutely report, "I will look at my draft and find its faults," and the novelists seem admirable for their toughness, though the big writing muscles those words expose give no evidence of authorial wisdom in the pumped-up novelist. This kind of boat-repairing mantra, "I will look at my work and find its faults," ignores the fact that what is before the novelist is a work of such large scale that it is both boat and river.

If, during your proud fault-finding you give first priority to locating the problems in your early draft, you will correct and correct the draft, repairing and repairing the boat (the embodiment of your controlled technical skills) before you have gazed into the extraordinary qualities of the river (the embodiment of your inventive capabilities always carrying you beyond what you can consciously control).

By such a method of correction, you proudly, willfully identify the flaws you have caused in your novel. By this method you are not involved in willingly entering your novel's flaw-transcending qualities. You have placed your will over the will of the work. You are outside the work, answering and inventorying, feeling assured you are addressing your novel's problems. You are not inside the work, questioning and inventing, feeling emboldened to explore your novel's possibilities.

It may seem that I'm recommending overthinking the processes of composing and revising. If we think too much we can't write a damn thing. I mean to recommend that inside their own work the writer can feel their way deeper past the processes of asking, "What feels wrong here?" Or, "What feels right here?" The writer can ask, "What feels marvelously right-wrong-right here?" and, so, always place themself inside the dualities of dynamic balance.

During the long commitment to their art, a writer might ask, "What is the altered instrument that—at this stage of my life—claims me?"

A mistake and the perfection of that mistake

I propose a really general distinction: that *work* is the phase at which you are reckoning with the familiar material before you (for instance, a poem of receptive and resistant memory; a story in the voice of an inarticulate narrator), and that *craft* is the phase at which you are transforming the worked material (for instance, the personal memory poem that has a misremembering poem of history inside; the inarticulate narrative with silences and deeper silences marking it).

In your composing process, do you almost never cleanly separate your *work* from your *craft?* Do you in your composing process make and then remake and craft and re-craft even from phrase to phrase, noun phrase to verb phrase, from sentence to sentence? And, when you take up the most significant stages of revision, are your concerns from draft to draft *crafting* concerns, because you feel that the *work* is already done?

In your wordwork how patient can you be in finding the word that expressively and rhythmically feels right *before* you do the wordcraft of welcoming the uncanny word that is wrong *and* right at the same moment?

In your wordwork how patient are you in identifying the concerted singular quality of the word you have written? In your wordcraft how bold are you in welcoming multiple, disconcerting qualities (as in the synesthetic conditions or the jarring sonic forces in the word you have written)?

With each draft of the passage before you, you move through phases of wordwork and wordcraft. Do you stop revising when you intuitively feel that what you planned in the wordwork has been fully transformed or even entirely undone by the wordcraft?

And, do you have a sense of how much the materials of your poem or story decide for you your balancing of working and crafting, your phases of working and crafting?

To what degree do you feel that all your jig inventions—"jigs," the broad term for the small and large devices that help the work of the hands—are ready-made and are now so characteristic of everyone else's craft that they have become your default equipment? Do you, for instance, eschew end-line punctuation in all your poems or quotation marks on all speech in all of your fiction no matter how absolutely different one story or one poem is from another? Was that choice you made a "workmanship of risk" choice—or a "workmanship of certainty" choice? To leave out the end-line punctuation or the speech-designating quotation marks will definitely require you to rework and recraft if only for the sake of affective and effective coherence and flow: some works will definitely be served by this choice you have made. Some works: *not*. And in a whole book: to put the end-line punctuation in one poem or the quotation marks in one story and to leave them out of a very different kind of story and poem—do you worry that that so-called inconsistency will mark your work as unsophisticated, out-of-the-mainstream, imperfect?

What is the degree to which the writer trusts the infinite possibilities created by the quasi-patterns of language relenting to and resisting order? What is the degree to which the writer trusts the infinite possibilities created by the quasi-patterns of language resisting and relenting to chaos? The equilibrist and the dynamist—let's assume both are always present in the mature artist—think and feel their way through these questions in their composing and revising choices.

Consider Francis Ponge's footnote on his prose poem "The Goat": "So the goat, like all creatures, is both a mistake and the perfection of that mistake; and hence pitiful and admirable, alarming but exciting all at once."

Feeling the grain of narrative occasion

For me there is great pleasure in working in the materials of first-person viewpoint in my stories and prose poems. If the first-person voice has orality as one of its clear values, I take pleasure in slowing myself down, conscientiously *working* to discover the narrative situation: who is this being told to; for what reason that is implicit in the speaker/listener situation; and on what occasion has this narrative emerged?

A natural part of a person's consciousness is what's going on out there in the world at large. This is called ethical anxiety.

To what degree is this covertly or overtly affecting characters? To what degree will it be organic to the work to acknowledge this?

You might say, "Mc, this obsessive concern with narrative situation—are you sure you don't care about all of that more than the reader cares?"

I'm not at all sure. A reader with no deep-structure experience of orality (I estimate that that is about ninety percent of twenty-first century American readers)—I worry that reader is, sadly, not my reader. I worry, and I go on.

I grew up immersed in oral culture and, so, this *work* of worrying out narrative situation is pleasurable for me. Even if the narrative situation will not ultimately be explicitly established in the story, I want the full childlike pleasure of feeling my way into the narrative situation before I begin the pleasurable adultlike phases of crafting.

Working to do something like perceiving narrative occasion is working to recognize duality—that *encounter of pain | encounter of beauty* sense, that *because of | despite of* sense, the awareness that illusion enfolds the so-called real.

If your workmanship reveals to you the familiar occasion that shapes your passage, craft a radically different occasion. If naming or renaming the occasion shaping your passage now requires that you revise the passage, do it.

What I'm asking is to acknowledge the strange joys of being artists *and* artisans.

The *artisan* patiently, fully takes in the material before her—the grain of this soft or hard wood, the particles of this dense or pliable clay, the harmonies and disharmonies in this kind of stone, the competing textures in this artificial or natural fiber—in order to reckon with it as a familiar wonder with rather amazing qualities of *reproducibility*. The *artist* patiently realizes the potentialities of the otherness and of the astounding *irreproducibility* inherent in the same material.

I really do believe that in the long term the writer impatient with the work phase will more slowly—perhaps too slowly—reckon with their own complex nature as an artisan.

I really do believe that in the long term the writer who is

impatient with the craft phase will more slowly—too slowly—realize their own otherness and rarity.

Shelter and the shit basket

The process of composing for me is an avoidance of style. The word style implies authorial decision-making and shaping.

My process of revising through many transformative drafts is growing acceptance that the wildnesses in the work can be released rather than tamed.

In all the arts, what gives me pleasure is how the thing itself—the sculpture, the dance, the music, the painting—asserts its own pleasure-taking, pleasure-making characteristics that the artist has respected and, as a result of that respect, has intensified.

I accept responsibility for the style a particular piece has discovered.

One reader described the style in my novel *One Kind Favor* as "antic exuberance." I like that description because it reflects a kind of art that decenters rather than centers and re-centers you in it.

I reread Rita Dove's *Thomas & Beulah* in order to learn from that profoundly crafted and workmanlike book of poems how to be a writer of a certain kind: the writer whose so-called style is inextractable from the work's "essence." Let's call it "essential style." One asks, "Is that Rita Dove inside those poems?" It is something different than the work of a writer (think of Ernest Hemingway or Cormac McCarthy) whose "style" is inextractable from the writer's will. Let's call it "intentional style." One asks, "Inside that Hemingway—is that a story?"

Thomas Berger writes that it is hardwired in humans that everything we make with our hands is a shelter: "The first necessity of life is shelter. Shelter against nature. The first sign of life is pain. It is within this bleak natural context that beauty is encountered. However it is encountered, beauty is always an exception, always *in despite of.*"

One could say that "style" is another word for the *kind* of shelter your work makes.

Have you made a ground nest—unwoven, perishable: a place for leaving?

Have you made an air nest—woven, meant to be permanent: a place for staying?

Have you made an empty nest—ruined, quiet, eerie?

Have you made a full nest—loud with eggs and fledglings—and does it have a shit basket on its rim? Many full nests have as part of their beauty a place for all the bird shit that would otherwise be on the floor of the nest. The shit has been moved to this little hanging basket; the basket has sometimes been flown away by the adult bird and dropped from the air. The shit basket is, depending on your perspective, a beautiful piece of work, as worthy of studying as some nests are.

For many writers it is not easy to imagine the one reader for work that is, by its nature, an impermanent thing, not made for all posterity, but a record of a moment.

If you are a certain kind of receptive reader, the one reader writers too seldom imagine for an individual work, you appreciate these improvisations not because they attach to a bigger picture, a full-blown poem or prose, but because they enact life's ramshackle, temporary structures.

The writer in readiness

I've come to believe it's the best possible thing for anyone who presumes to make art to place yourself in uncertainties, to be in over your head, to realize that the work is asking you to rise above your limitations.

Practice the recognition that what you are making eludes you. You are inviting it to have its elusive separateness, strangeness, its otherness.

When composing, ask yourself:

> What moment is before me?
> What transformative moment is before me?
> What contracting | expanding transformative moment?
> What engaging | estranging transformative moment?
> What self-compounding | self-extinguishing transformative moment?
> What time-reforming | time-deforming transformative moment?
> What harmonious | disharmonious transformative moment?

If a moment is mysterious, enigmatic and does not illuminate the primary drama, then you can let it be expansive so that the reader is saying, "What is this? Where is it going?"

I have heard novelists mourn that they have the whole draft in hand but cannot crisply state the theme. In some cases, the request for theme comes from well-meaning family members or friends, who have made clear they do not read novels though they like to give them as presents. In some cases, an agent or book editor has asked the novelist for this thematic summation—an agent or editor with a long history of advising every novelist to imagine a reader who values depiction (i.e, the well-designed inert architectural model) over description (i.e., the lived-in architecture of a building occupied by human, animal, and vegetal life).

Sometimes writers get blocked by The Theme Dilemma.

Facing this dilemma, avoid efficiently focusing upon something that will illustrate one narrow thematic case the story is constructing or one superficial effect for which the story strives. Explore the *story* that breathes life into ideas and thought experiments. Feel how story *transforms* and *enacts* what is usually *transacted* and *imparted.*

During the revision process, a writer is helped by challenging themself to scrutinize (with pleasure) their habits of presenting the efficient "establishing observation" in their work. The temptation to do this occurs most at the bridging moments in the story, those moments when the storyteller is trying to smoothly move from one story element to the next. And, of course, a story beginning is a bridging moment since it is moving us from a title to an initiating moment.

It's a questionable writing habit, repeatedly writing the establishing observation, because it reinforces for the reader patterns of observation that are orienting, ordering, and controlling; it does not move the reading experience past mere transaction.

We sometimes seem to ask the writer to establish a pattern-identifying sensibility in the very first moments of the reading experience, and then to offer in the next-to-last moments the reward of observing the last stages of a pattern cohering. According to the futurist and entrepreneur Ray Kurzweil, in our era we have defined intelligence as expertise in recognizing patterns, in training our minds to expertly curate. Is it possible that poems and stories can immerse the reader in this complex pattern-recognizing and in a pattern-disrupting and even pattern-obscuring experience? It is possible, by my reckoning, that we do not have to choose one method over another, since there is opportunity, particularly in the desinent moment of the work, for the reader to recognize shape persisting and shape perishing.

People going nowhere

Sometimes we have a feeling that the reader can't handle too much chaos, so we try to compartmentalize. Instead, ask yourself why the stage of the work isn't more dynamically crowded.

It's often at the beginning of the novel that this rigid control takes root. In what I call the "Noah's Ark structure," the entire draft has scenes where characters appear two by two in well-controlled scenes that do not at all oblige the author to accommodate the complexities of polylogue. Why are there never three people in the same scene, and why never one person in that scene remembering two or three not present? Are characters presented two by two because the book requires it, or has the writer needed to create a structure that gives control over the drama such that there's no need to think about the interpenetrative drama?

A trialogue is inherently unstable. The characters move in and out of chaos. One party is constantly ingressing—speaking out loud to herself—another is progressing—speaking to a larger audience—and a third is both progressing and ingressing—speaking to the self and to others outside the setting; it is this person who is likely the alpha in the trialogue. The dynamics of trialogue are greatly influenced by setting, which grounds or ungrounds the different parties to differing degrees—one person already departing; one actually there; and one constantly departing and returning. But to create this rhythm, extended scene is necessary.

Extended scene reveals aspects of characters that manifest only when they are together for a long time. In our own lives, we are frequently with someone longer than we would have wished. We would like to bail, but we can't. We run out of words. We only talk around what we would have talked about. Then a third party arrives that makes it more difficult for both of us.

Anaïs Nin, portraying surrogate pain—the pain one feels for and with another—often uses scene in which people indirectly or directly say quite clumsy things to each other, quite artificial things that are the unnatural expressions of people acting on feeling and not thought, or trying to move past acting on thought into communicating feelings, particularly pain and pleasure. (The Welsh word that Nin uses to describe this form of dialogue that moves toward intimacy is "furrawn.")

Extended scene is often most accurately dreamlike and real when it shows us characters immobilized, talking with each other while immobilized, trying to break through, making the effort to put aside the goal of "getting somewhere"—putting such goals aside as poetry does—in order to be fully present to both the freeing and the failing core of their relationship.

More and more in recent years a great scene in fiction reads to me like a poem: in its very form on the page, dialogue is vaguely stanzaic, after all; its rhythmic flow, the scene's syncopated vocal music gives the unstressed beat its "sinking back" grace as it would in a poem; in its radical respect for how people, in conversation with voices inside and outside, with the voices of the past, present, and future, unlearn our usual serviceable words, unlearn our habituated dialogue transactions, and, instead, hold ourselves to the ground of intimacy: the absence of "structure hunger," which is the term for our need for stimulus in an ordered and orienting form.

In many works of fiction that have a great claim on me there is dialogue that immobilizes me as a reader. Since it acutely, memorably shows me people going nowhere, it prevents me from thinking, What mission, what goal is this scene advancing in the overall work?

Melody & groove, groove & melody

I do sincerely believe that almost all of the energies of plot are replaceable in story. Still, I believe the storyteller whose work even mildly suspends elements of plot must discover in the work what will replace plot energy with another energy every bit as dynamic.

The pleasures of working with plot include satisfying questions—What is wrong with him/her/them? What is wrong that is about to get worse, or get better? Where did the wrongness start and how will it or how can it end or at least change?—that lead to unfolding their apparent outcomes: loud, spectacular dramas—*spectacles*—ways of becoming. The difficult pleasures of working with plot or conflict include reconciling the matter of paradox—What is wrong and is at the self-same moment right about them? What is exasperatingly, beautifully, unchangeable about them?—that lead to presenting quiet moments of *drama* and revealing their invisible subtle outcomes—ways of being.

I find it is consoling to hear the "take" of James Brown's "Love Don't Love Nobody" on the reissue of *Messing with the Blues* in which the finished song and the take have been published together. On the take, about twenty-five seconds in, Brown stops his amazing tailpipe-dragging-sparks-flying singing because the sound engineer breaks in to convey a message from someone—I'm pretty sure it is God—saying, "That was a good start, man—make it more of a melodic thing—you sang the hell out it—but just a little more melody." It is the kind of thing on live performance recordings that you can hear Brown telling his own band musicians in a way that makes clear he is also reminding himself: honor thy wolf and thy wolf's mother, but don't lose the melody.

You already know this: any specific advice I offer you will be welcomed and not welcomed, invaluable and useless, serious and foolish. If my ill-advised advice will provide a way for you to re-enter your draft and ask from within it how to more deeply respect its paradoxes, I regret | celebrate those blessed | cursed conditions.

Be in the dynamic condition of doubt as you compose and revise. Futility is the generative starting place for many powerful works of art.

Inviting overwhelming engagement, estrange.

Inviting overwhelming estrangement, engage.

Iris and ichor

The reason art is so counterintuitive is that we find connection in estrangement.

One way in which writers often miss the opportunity to give the wolf tone its due is in our unconscious and conscious efforts to eliminate or suppress the most estranging qualities of the speaker or the subject of the poem, of the characters or character relationships in the story, of the narrative sensibility, of the work's presentation of the milieu. Writers learn, often despite themselves, how to use the "wolf eliminator" and the "wolf suppressor" to restrain the offenses that are, after all, natural to certain works. In composing, if the poet will not play inappropriately with his dolls and, at times, with his own shit, then estranging, playful, grating, fine poems like Russell Edson's or James Tate's never get written. In revising, if the prose writer always stops the character's progressions of observation or processes of thought at the threshold of the unspeakable, then work like Ian McEwan's and Doris Lessing's is not possible. Who reads Sherwood Anderson's visceral, unforgettable "Death in the Woods" without the thought that you wish you had never read it? It goes too far. It goes too far in its depiction of the most revolting images. If you have just read "Death in the Woods," and then you read other works by Sherwood Anderson, benign enough but always having that hyssop-soaked sponge in them—then—while there is still a little vomit in your mouth—you are ready for D.H. Lawrence's *Women in Love*.

My life always feels richest when I'm immersed in intimate experience of dark and luminous beauty. I'm passionate about flower gardening because it reminds me that inside wonder is horror, inside horror is wonder: a foxglove blossom from which stinging bees emerge; a dying, then dissolving and collapsing iris from which ichor pours.

We say certain kinds of work are "difficult" and, sometimes, that is our way of saying they are failures in their efforts to present complex dark and luminous beauty that the artist simply could not meet on its own terms without *radically relenting* to its strangenesses. It's my experience that when a person in the lecturer's priestly robes—a person like me—calls the artist a "failure," in most cases that person is simply projecting onto the artist his shame about failing to meet the work on its own terms. It's my experience that when people name a difficult work—the instrument itself—as a failure, they are often engaged in a conscientious process of trying to reckon with the mystery of how often it is perfectly natural for the boldest art to have a persistent "wolf tone" that will cause it to tremble between failing and, as Samuel Beckett expressed it, "failing better."

Discussions of "the uncanny" confront issues of whether the work is, finally, just one awful "wolfy area" or a well-grounded reading experience haunted by wolves. Discussions of "duende" confront this issue, as well as discussions of "the unspeakable" and of "paradox" and of "gestalt."

The one reader

My readers, plural—my readers, monstrously plural—my enemy army—in the dialogue between me and my work, I want you out of the way. Writing one flawed page of something vaguely resembling literature's gift of the luminous abyss—well, it's already the hardest thing I'm ever going to do. And the more of you in the way, the worse it goes for me. No wonder I try not to think of all of you when I compose. No wonder I resent you when I revise.

Instead of the default mode of referring to *readers*, I suggest a simple thought experiment: contemplate *the one reader.*

Think about it from within one particular piece in your body of work. How far can you go in characterizing that one reader for whom that one work really exists?

I want to emphasize this: I'm not inviting you to generalize about the one reader for all your work; in the whole body of your work there might be commonalities in the one reader, but this kind of reckoning is done best one moment at a time, in my opinion. If a writer is patient with what Heidegger calls the "letting-dwell" moments ("das Verweilen," in *Poetry, Language, Thought*) of composing and revising, she stays that world of the work, and it stays to reveal her relationship to it. Heidegger says of poetry: "The work holds open the Open of the world."

Many of us, at various stages of drafting, read aloud to ourselves, not as some form of practice for an imagined performance, but in a kind of "testing" of the material, in the effort to engage with it more deeply or on different terms. Is a writer who does this, reading to One Reader who is himself? If so, is he suffering from what Walter Kerr called "delusions of adequacy"? If I am still a writer who is a Reader-in-Training, is it better for me as I read aloud to summon a resistant, receptive, reflexive reader far more dynamic than I?

The writer who is a resistant reader must question that persisting condition.

The writer who is not a *radically* receptive reader must question that condition.

The generative—wildly, obscenely, radically—resistant reader

A resistant audience is the default audience many poets and fiction writers imagine because, after all, their most disciplined and ineluctable early training was in the extremely rigid forms of essay writing that supposedly taught the young, bright, alive writer to make assertions and construct arguments acceptable to a large audience of desiccated, dim, dying adults whose flaccid brains could be effectively compromised by a shapely opening sentence: the thesis statement. The one reader—the teacher who had given the assignment, let us call him Mr. Sawdust, and who represented his generation of Sawdusts—was certainly present in the young reader's mind in many dynamic ways. The writer, in varying degrees of self-consciousness, imagined what Mr. Sawdust simply would not accept.

Are the readers for your work the descendants of the Sawdust clan? Are they alert to error above all else? Have they made you as a writer error-avoiding in both your processes of composing and revising?

How generative are those resistant readers to us in each new moment of our lives as writers? I ask it as a sincere question. Many of us who still write for those resistant readers have found it valuable, through time, to allow our relationship to the Sawdusts to devolve to the ur-relationship with Mr. Sawdust, to go further in imagining that one resistant reader who just might be surprisingly, wildly, obscenely, radically resistant.

We'll call this reader Mr. Spunkwater. You are creating something rhythmic in nature, already you are on all fours upon the labyrinthine wen of trace and track that just might be a poem, but because you have some notion that you had meant to or mean to travel somewhere transported by plot or theme, it just might be a prose. It is not going well, and, though you are trying not to think of the Sawdust clan, you have hardly been successful. You are composing inside this one unique emergence of this one world. You are experiencing translucence, a "shining-through": a something is appearing in the wen (a word for the naturally inscrutable language that nature makes in sand where a lizard has swished its tail or in the underside of bark where beetles have written metrically). You cannot be alone with the magic of it, though you wish you could.

The experience you are writing about—a kind of cute thing about you and your umbrella—is not deepening, not getting less silly. You believe that what might occur is the illumination of something Eternal, but what occurs is the trans-illumination of something Ephemeral. You can feel the disappointment, the implicit condemnation of the Sawdust clan. Rimbaud, Verlaine, Baudelaire—how they hated the Sawdust clan! You are in their company though they are not coming to mind. You will censor yourself at this crucial point—or you will liberate yourself. In order to be liberated you might wish to consider whether the resistant reader who is already present in this particular work has been actually provoked and punctured instead of merely prodded. You have written badly but you have not risked allowing it to be atrocious.

If you now imagine Mr. Spunkwater with greater particularity, his despicable love for the hieratic mode and his Kipling fixation and his confusing hate-love for the decorative in language, you revise this line: "Puddles receded, recoiled from my wet feet and around me everything was in flux." You write, "Puddles receded, nay recoiled from my once-wet feet and around me everything was a-something, achirp, aflutter." A crime committed against Mr. Spunkwater is a commitment to the unprofound. You have not made these ongoing changes (let's call them "improvisations" and hold off calling them "revisions") from outside the work.

Mr. Spunkwater was present there with you in the mystery of it. Possibly, in what you are writing, there is delight and pleasure in being inside the work and allowing its own spitting energies to most fully insult and injure Mr. Spunkwater.

It might just be a good thing if the one writer making this poem prose is energized by the way this one work itself wishes to violate the one reader's—Mr. Spunkwater's—sensibilities in every way possible.

If not, why not?

I want to come to terms with both what the reader is receptive to and what the reader is resistant to. I often will read a sentence and ask myself, "Mc, are you receptive to this sentence or are you resistant to it?" Since the normal assumption is that we are making sentences that the reader will be receptive to, it's quite compelling to think that many readers are excited by exactly the kind of prose they are resistant to. Many readers who think they want to be engaged also wish to be estranged. If the work will not give them the opportunity to be estranged, it will be merely engaging. The marvelous thing about Beckett, for instance, is that he is constantly estranging us, and we're amazed that we're engaged. But this is life at its richest. Life is full of these moments of receptivity and resistance, of engagement and estrangement.

I pictured for my story collection *57 Octaves Below Middle C* a reader who has a seriously disturbed mind, who appears maybe to everyone around her or him quite normal, a person aware that their mind does not work like the "normal" mind, a person who readily welcomes not only estrangement but repugnance. When I was far enough into my novel *At the Gate of All Wonder*, I imagined a reader who was more delighted by the language nature makes than the language humans make—the language the birds make, that trees make in wind, that creatures make in their burrows. For *Hyssop*, I pictured the one reader who wishes for all language to act like prayer.

In *One Kind Favor*, the character Acker is the embodiment of the writer Kathy Acker who was in her moment identified as a punk writer whose work had many, many qualities that were off-putting, that are accurately describable as obscene, as repugnant. This was part of her aesthetic, to write her prose in such a way that it had raw, unfinished edges. It not only skidded into chaos, but it thoroughly resided there. Her great masterpiece, in my opinion, was a book called *Blood and Guts in High School.* It has obscene graffiti throughout, and the storytelling resists you. Reading it, you are coming to terms with a form of chaos that is daring you to say, "Have I at any point in my life welcomed in this kind of experience? If I have not, why not?"

Your work's own true nature

In discussing categories of reader I've made liberal use of the terms of rhetoric that refer to receptive, resistant, and reflexive reader. The last of these is the most mysterious.

Does the reader for a particular work live inside the work?

In each stage of the dialogue between the writer and the work has the writer relented to the reader who is already there?

When you have spoken with someone about how you were carried by the work beyond your intentions, you have asked yourself, "How did *that* happen?" when inside you already feel that the more pertinent question is, *Who* made *that* happen?

A writer who finds the one reader in that zone will be terribly at risk. Do you want to be so much at risk?

To do it you might wish to have the wrong tool in your hand (what in philosophy is called Muller's Ratchet, a broken tool that can only loosen or tighten and cannot do both); if you are King Oliver, you might wish to have a derby or a plunger over the mouth of your cornet. If you are Bob Dylan, having mastered the acoustic folk-protest poem, you might choose a Stratocaster and too much reverb in order to give the resistant reader of this particular work, "Stuck Inside of Mobile with the Memphis Blues Again," an accumulation of agitants. You are moving the receptive reader of this particular work past what he thinks he needs to what he desires that overrides those needs. You are addressing the stranded person you have found inside this one work—a stranded person who shares certain aspects in common with the artist formerly known as Bob Dylan. You are offering something transformative to The One Reader who thought he was your True Audience of One until this thing, a something that is neither folk nor rock, and that presents the conversation between you and your new Muse this way: "And I say, 'O, come on now, you know you know about my debutante.' And she says, 'Your debutante just knows what you need—but I know what you want.'"

To what degree do you acknowledge the presence of the resistant, the receptive, and the reflexive reader all present in the work as it unfolds before you? And do you push beyond one-dimensional perceptions of that reader? Finally: do you construct this crisis of audience or do you find it created in the work—and do you welcome it?

Do you as a writer have to make excuses for honoring your work's own true nature? No. Do you have to be rigorously honest with yourself about that question? Yes.

I *can* imagine one resistant reader with whom I have both a divine and demonic relationship. It is harder for me to imagine readers, plural, who welcome both my grasping and my groping.

Picturing one reader means humbly acknowledging to yourself as a writer that certain things you write are just not for everyone.

I like to encounter art that exists in the culture but that resists that culture's fundamental values. In the Philadelphia Art Museum, I found myself mesmerized by the Soutine paintings. In his letters to others, Soutine acknowledges that he could make neither a controlled straight nor a curved line. He just couldn't do it. You look at his portraits of people, portraits in which the people look like praying mantises or melting toads, and you see how they do not at all reveal likenesses but surprising trembling othernesses. Looking at them, I can't image who would want to have an artist render their Likeness when the artist could render their Other.

I would like as a writer to meet the characters on their own terms instead of making them fit my terms. I would like the reader to experience in my novels the receptivity and resistance that the reader experiences daily as a part of life's surprising and disruptive richness. A boring life is a life of well-controlled ease and successful avoidance of conflict; boring art recapitulates that design. As far as I can tell, a life of fullness is not a life in which one completed experience follows another; art that has fullness has no discernable completeness. The characters I write about have lives of spilling and overspilling instead of lives that pour forth in a measured, controlled way.

My readers—my readers—

It is not good between me and the whole gang of you. It never has been. It never will be.

I have left you so many times in my life as a writer. And every time you have immediately taken up with other writers: Walt Whitman (always on the make, o comarado) and John Berryman (pouring pages out for you in the clutches of a wild infatuation) and Sylvia Plath (offering you fresh strychnine pie) and the un-gulaged Russians and those stringy-bearded eleventh century Chinese painter poets. You turn on a dime and go to them. That's how promiscuous you are. When, in my own mewling, pathetic ways, I have asked to come back to you, you have abandoned poor Akhmatova and Shiki and Captain Robert Bly, and have welcomed me back.

Why? I don't know

I do, despite myself, care about you, beloved readers, enemy army, monstrously plural.

Because—

Readers can be won despite themselves. They can realize that overriding what they thought they needed, which was engagement, the story, the prose itself, has provided something they desired beyond their understanding, which was the push and pull of estrangement-engagement.

Intense pleasure generates intense gratefulness *if* the writer permits it, *if* the writer brings fullness (that satisfying unlocking instant) to the moments that might have offered only completeness (that superficially satisfying latch-closing instant).

Acknowledging the gifts of co-consciousness, sustain the silences.

Acknowledging the gifts of subconscious processes, crowd the darknesses.

As I was working away, intent on making a presentable, powerful, sensible, and purposeful lecture, I took a break to walk into a patch of our garden where the balloon flowers needed pinching—this is my life at middle age when pinching off is an essential life skill—anyway, with the very first quite enjoyable pinch, I was stung on my head and hands by hornets—exquisite and instantaneous fiery pain that gave me an intimate reminder of my own unique ways of responding to what finds me that I never sought. Immediately afterwards I had pleasure in remembering them calling me by name as they attacked: "Mmmmmmack! Mmmmmmmack! Mmmmmack-mmmmmaack-mmmmack!" And I felt pleasure in the wonder of the pain waking up all my senses so that the cold water I ran over my hands felt hot; the water sounded different pouring out of the spigot; it smelled and tasted *better*; and there was odd, fine pleasure later in learning my marvelous enemy-angel's name, "white-faced hornets."

I experienced the beautiful, I experienced the beautiful in the form of a swarm. Kantian philosophy has described it this way: "...the feeling of the beautiful is a reflexive judgment, *singular* (though it claims universality), *immediate*, and *disinterested*. It arises only from one faculty of the soul, that of pleasure and pain, and it takes place on the occasion of a form."

The attentive witness

Every waking and sleeping moment, we must be present to the world around us.

The gift of art is to be present to the moment. Ordinarily we may not be present to something like seeing a man look in a window at his own reflection, but in art, we can pay attention, see what the outcome is going to be.

If the character has a preoccupation with her clothing—she pulls her sleeve closer to her body—then what is the outcome of that? A gesture that recurs evolves in its significance. A man standing at the window is, at first, just looking at his reflection, but later in the novel, he is looking through himself.

Gestures are the manifestation of expression for which there are no words. We remember from a formative part of our life phatic, preverbal communication—the child's body expressing what it needs. In your early drafts, notice what the smallest gestures illuminate, then work from there back to the main dramas.

Become a student of the details that represent fate—fatidic detail.

Find the *transforming detail*, the detail in which the character's mystery begins. Not the detail that *identifies* the character, but the detail that *mystifies* and sometimes becomes the very reason for writing a story—to reside within a mystery for twenty or two hundred pages.

My trust in these processes is essential to my discipline as an attentive witness, by which I mean my craft as a storyteller. A storyteller, after all, is a watcher always looking for new methods to recognize human mysteries in their most paradoxical manifestations.

We all have secrets that will make their way out of us, no matter our efforts to shut them out. You've experienced this process of *educing* when you've tried mightily not to laugh, but a seizure of laughter has overcome you at the most inappropriate moment possible. You've experienced this when the right conditions have elicited from you exactly the wrong words, which you insist are "totally out of character." Under the pressure of an extreme emotion, you've told a story about yourself that is a fiction in every particular yet is the hidden essence of who you are. You understand that a person can live a long life of answering his own needs without ever having committed to answering his own desires, his own wish for experiences that offer more than necessities can fulfill. A person's hidden desires are often his ghosts, pressed far down but making themselves more and more urgently known.

The superabundance of any force produces its opposite. If you exaggerate what is central to your own condition, what will emerge is the exact opposite. The extreme of self-loving leads to self-loathing. The extreme of wealth becomes impoverishment. The extreme of engagement becomes indifference.

In storytelling this is one of the forms of *enantiodromia*: taken at its extreme, any essential trait of an individual will arrive to meet the individual in its opposite form—a double. A writer who is conscientiously honest with himself about his failures will find he is writing a story about a person who is dishonest with himself about his failures. A person not wishing to change will be met by a force of nature ready to transcend dormancy.

Art places the reader *inside* the envelope of darkness where the envelope of light opens, places the reader *inside* the envelope of light where the envelope of darkness opens.

The body of the swarm

Most of us do acknowledge that our human consciousness is almost never singular. A person's individual consciousness is made more ordered or chaotic according to The Companion Within and The Companion Nearby: the companion not physically present but unmistakably existing within one, and the companion physically present and near. At most moments both companions are actively shaping the focus of a person's attention through the tug of war in which the person is resisting the other's viewpoint and relenting to it.

We live in a compounded sensibility in which we glide readily from the experience of the "I" to the "we" to the "they" and "us"; we still have the child learner inside us, the one who felt a fully alive somatic response to the stories that were read to them, who felt each word as if through the skin and flesh of the adults sitting so close, of the other child or children crowding in.

It's understood that for all of us co-consciousness occurs more readily in some settings than in others, in some social circumstances more than in others, more observably in some historical moments, and in some cultures and subcultures than in others. This is true for the islands in Sarah Orne Jewett's *The Country of the Pointed Firs*. Two settings in particular are places where the narrator is twice removed from what is familiar, and her own singular consciousness is dislodged. The character's ways of looking—Jewett's expansive presentation of harmonious and disharmonious co-consciousness—provide the sense of increasing wonder and excitement that replaces the energy of plot.

The higher the degree of co-consciousness, the more there is accommodation in so-called realistic fiction to acknowledge the irreal, to observe the world in which the *as is* and the *as if* interpenetrate. If it is invited into the work, the dynamic conflict of the *as is* and the *as if* conditions reminds the reader of the mystery of blindsight. That is the word for explaining the phenomenon of the blind spot. Neuroscientists call blindsight our way of "more or less accurately" filling in the visual field around a blind spot. And isn't the experience of blindsight essential to our satisfying, pleasurable experience of all art?

Depending upon one's degree of permeability, of suggestibility, a person can experience the "failure to correctly identify body parts as one's own"—somatoparaphrenia. Competition rowers surely experience this. Dancers in the frame experience it. A family many years at the same table. A traveler in unfamiliar circumstances will draw their wallet out of their own pocket according to the will of the pickpocket. Our consciousness is "selectively permeable," according to the philosopher Rober Nozick, and it matters to our sense of narrative to discover the shifting degrees of permeability in individual persons and in the relationship of co-conscious persons.

The dramatic power of story resides in characters' co-conscious experiences of what is. In such a story, so much more depends on the dramas of looking than on the dramas of doing. Perhaps that's because in a work that commits to co-consciousness, decision-making and objective assessment become pleasurably impossible efforts. The *we* sensibility has redefined each observer's autonomy. Consider, for example, ardent love: under that influence, the writing can offer superabundance (Robert Nozick uses that term in his discussion of the "holiness of the everyday") in its observations, in its outlook and inscape, the eye expansively focusing on the outer and the inner regions.

It is possible to construe many plots of co-consciousness that occur directly in the passages of observation, particularly the ones arriving through co-conscious desire (the plot of ardent love): the "I" wants deeper into the "we" consciousness and then wants it to continue; the "I" wants out of the "we" consciousness and wants it to cease; the "we" wants to enlarge the "we" to three or more, and the "I" resists. Perhaps this struggle is what Roland Barthes referred to "an Other-ache" in *A Lover's Discourse.*

Pass the biscuits, in silence

What we do not express matters as much as what we do. Let's say this Thanksgiving our eccentric but beloved cousin has brought, once again, his special homemade biscuits, a very large basket of inedible biscuits. As he does every Thanksgiving, he asks, "Want me to pass 'em around again?" and his question is met with silence, then a nervous remark from one of us about weight-watching, then others joining in about gaining so much weight during the holidays. We feel that the little island of silence is affectionate, that it increases connection to our cousin and, so, it increases love among all of us at the table who love him. This is engaging silence.

Let's say a little time passes and he mutters, "I'm sendin' 'em around again now." We can feel that the answering silence is still engaging, but it lasts a beat longer before anything else is said. There is a subtext: O, dear cousin, we sure wish, just for a second, we could disappear, eliminate ourselves from this familiar tableau, not have to hurt your feelings either directly or indirectly. This is an erasing silence.

And now, as everyone is finishing eating, our cousin says, a little indignantly, "Last call for my biscuits." He has done this every Thanksgiving. Every Thanksgiving, he has brought the biscuits no one has been able to eat. He has eternally taken offense. And this Thanksgiving he has taken offense again. And, for a moment, so have we. The silence of the group is the longest one yet. It is a protesting silence.

It is a protesting silence; but later, after we have all kissed and hugged him with genuine affection, and have not declined his invitation to leave the biscuits for us to have as snacks, after he has gone home, we will remember it as a protesting silence that was, at the very same moment, an erasing silence, and an engaging silence.

Sometimes, two people have such uncanny harmony that their processes of instantiation, of completing and filling in and refining and reframing each other's expressions, are as marvelously nonsense-making as the dialogue between a child and her dolls, a child and her imaginary friends, a child utterly infatuated with another child. We observe this in longstanding friendships and marriages and other kinds of extended partnerships. I have had the opportunity to directly observe the co-conscious singing of people in institutional settings, including a maximum-security prison, in which the communication of inmates in the same cell for many years was marked by jargon and coded language, punctuated by deeply intimate silences. These "silential relations" defy identifiable meaning while creating and intensifying our sense of connection. Singing writers understand the ways in which this speech presented in a literary work can be the cause of fearful wonder for the reader.

When we read the work of a master storyteller like Willa Cather, who presents so many iterations of silence in the scenes and the narration of *O Pioneers!* and *The Professor's House* and *My Mortal*

Enemy, we are thankful for her extraordinary respect for both the scale of the expressible and the scale of the inexpressible. When our cousin spoke aloud about his infernal Thanksgiving biscuits, he was expressing so many things for which he has no words; when we were rendered speechless by his actions, gestures, and his speech, we felt the full scale of what we, too, can never express.

Any writer who has ever had any musical training knows that where silences land—whether overt silences that manifest themselves in space breaks, covert silences that have to do with the ending of this sentence and the beginning of the next, silences that are made very definite by chaptering, and silences that occur in a pre-climactic moment and a post-climactic moment—change the terms of engagement. Poets, of course, learn how to trust silence so much that they have a sense of the pressure sonically on either side of a silence, the created gap that has energy, the leap that has energy.

On a normal writing day for me, I start my morning by copying out Bashō or Neruda. Then I'll begin writing. After about half an hour, I'll blow on my harmonica for half an hour and specifically try to be inside the blues that I love, Delta blues, especially that gospel-inflected Delta blues. Then I'll write for an hour and a half, then blow on the harp. The harp is a way for me to be playing the blues while also carrying in my mind what I'm writing, so if I'm trying to play something that Big Walter Horton played, in which he was imitating a Tommy Dorsey tune bended into the blues, then I'm paying attention to where there's a very definite silence, a breathing silence, in which the player breathes into the harp, but there's no effort to make a note. Those forms of silences are constantly changing the terms of engagement. I know it sounds like I've thought all this through and have some mastery over it. I don't.

I've always trusted incoherence above coherence. It didn't

surprise me to find in many tragedies that the hero should always be more incoherent than coherent. Take King Lear. Lear begins in a kind of incoherent rage against his daughters and, as the play progresses, he becomes more incoherent; his soliloquies, when you read them carefully, make no sense. Lear's dilemma is that he has no words for what he feels. He is constantly up against the inexpressible.

The voice of The All

The "we" voice in tribal omniscience is a form of co-consciousness often inherently incoherent and chaotic because it is trying to be the voice for everyone. The reader feels almost immediately how irreal that is. That is, it is something that is real—we've heard it. We recognize it at first as the real-unreal. When someone uses it and sustains the use of it, it becomes more irreal as we listen.

My definition of irreal is more or less based on distinctions made by the fiction writer Julio Cortazar and by the poet Francis Ponge.

The *real* presents—supposedly—things and events as they are knowable, and asks us to recognize them as "reality." Sentences presenting the *real* make sense, and invite comprehension of *meaning*. "In the small pen the lamb nudged me with its ears."

The *surreal* presents—supposedly—things and events as unrecognizable and unknowable as seen from a certain angle or altered sensibility; the surreal asks us to acknowledge something *marvelous* and meaning-defying existing underneath or over accepted "reality." Sentences presenting the *surreal* often make nonsense-sense, and invite prehension (the something-there sensation). "The pre-lamb eared a pre-other me in our post-small pre-pen."

The *irreal* presents—supposedly—things and events as knowable yet barely recognizable as seen from a "normal" sensibility. We respond to the irreal as the *elusive real* that is both meaning-making and meaning-defying. Sentences presenting the *irreal* often make sense-nonsense and invite conflicted comprehension. "In the close pen with the lamb—ears soft—I felt—the lamb felt—a—what?—a small nudging premonition."

Why do I say "supposedly"? Because such definitions are only supposedly helpful in understanding distinctions in forms of consciousness.

In my novel *One Kind Favor*, the "we" is the narrative voice of the tribe of the small community of Cord, which knows its own so well that it can confidently tell—and can widely and accurately surmise—the town's past, present, and future stories. The voice is the chord of the town's many voices, the ones present and the ones long absent. As in most first-person plural voices, the voice has a root note, which comes from the town's storyteller—in this case, Union Vedder, a ghostly presence who has listened for so long that residents of the town who can never actually see him know he is there.

A community in which people still use "we" when talking about their own beloveds and outcasts and enigmatic figures and mythologized heroes and antagonists is a community still making the unconscious effort to cohere and to care. That "we" voice as easily falls into registers of indifference and cruel judging as it rises to self-questioning timbres of love and failed loving.

Tribal omniscience may also take the form of the absolute rules of some "tribes" occurring in written form (explicit instructions for behavior, terms of contract, rules for debate or battle or the aftermath of them, etc.) and spoken form (warnings by the guard at the gate, the judge's oral instructions to the jury, the funeral director's guidance to the pallbearers, etc.). In some instances, the rules are designed for a member of the tribe; in other instances, the rules are designed for the outsider. They have been compressed in order to be perfectly memorable. They are firm, restrained, jurisdictional. The rules are written in a voice that is human and mechanical.

Encountering inerrant rules, the reader remembers the story of their own tribe's explicit prohibitions, the limitations of its moral framework, and/or the limitless possibilities of that moral framework. The reader forms a picture of the rule-makers: an impersonal "we" that represents The All through many generations; a "we" represented by a specific spokesperson (a scribe, for instance) or spokespersons (multiple authors, as in The Declaration of Independence) *speaking for the all with the voice of The All.*

How does a "we" narrator make itself? One of the things I've come to believe is that autopoiesis, which is how a sentence makes itself, how any expression actually makes itself, is something that we always have the opportunity to be contemplating.

My experience of most storytellers is they ask first of the work they are composing, "What is it saying?" But my impulse has always been, "What is it singing?" With anything I write, if I can value its singing, I can find in it the way to value its saying.

I do try to feel my way in, push my thoughts back, then think my way in, allowing a constant flux in both my manner of composing and revising.

I think the temptation when you're writing prose is to create a push and glide effect in language, language that gets you from here to there, that introduces this idea or this character, that moves you into this space, this setting, and grounds you there, that orients you in time and serves in moving you forward through the story. That's one way of composing. Another way of composing is to write a sentence and to really live inside that sentence, to pay attention to it—what its sonic values are, what the characteristics of its autopoiesis are—before you allow yourself to write the next sentence, and the next. When you revise, instead of saying, "How is this sentence helping the reader push and glide through the work?" you ask yourself, "How is this sentence shifting the reader's intimate experience toward radical decentering?" How is it a thing of slender passing beauty, a sentence that will—if you will be inside of it for just a second more, no matter what your inclination as a reader—be an experience dark and luminous on its own terms?

If you're revising in terms of the push and glide, revision is asking you to change structural things: chaptering, space breaks, etc. But if you are revising sentence by sentence, you're being invited to create a different form of chaos than in the previous draft.

Co-consciousness, this matter of the see-er transformed into see-ers, is complicated. Willa Cather, the master of the witness narrator (a viewpoint character with *incomplete* information about characters, events, and the background of the story he or she tells) and of the forms of co-consciousness unlocked by that particular form of narrative, was unafraid of the complications. Cather's works take pains to establish the *incompleteness* of the stories told by visitors, and somehow this gives the narration more authority rather than less.

But it is intimidating. No wonder most of our literature gives so little attention to co-consciousness. Writers mostly avoid that complicated aspect of the human drama in order to fix on the task of getting one character's one consciousness to be authentic in its reactive and responsive observations. (I use here Robert Nozick's distinction between "reaction" and "response": "A *reaction* is a small piece of you reacting to a small piece of the situation by selection from a small and preset number of stereotypical actions.... In a full *response*, a large part of you responds to a large part of the situation by selection from a large range of nonstereotyped actions.")

In some cases, as a manner of presenting consciousness in multiple forms, we gravitate toward the kinds of omniscience in which various individual consciousnesses will be serially presented. That's a choice that is fine.

But. It's not the same thing, of course.

Many great teachers in history, including that great Christian, Hindu, Buddhist, Transcendentalist Thoreau, have observed that the very essence of what we call "sacred" is the void a human is freed into when their concept of an individual self dissolves and, with it, concepts of nonduality.

The writer does not often seek this form of beauty.

The reader does not often seek this form of beauty.

This form of beauty seeks the reader. This form of beauty seeks the writer.

Nesting order inside chaos, sensitize language's body.

Nesting chaos inside order, excite language's body.

On my father's side of the family, I grew up with these amazing oral storytellers whose stories never quite added up. The stories were gin-driven. They had a lot to do with getting a rise out of the audience. The stories had certain patterns to them, but they went off the rails very fast. They were long stories and, at the end of them, you would say to yourself, "What was that?" You could say that you had been present for singing and that the singing had been so spellbinding that almost from the first words you gave up any expectation of directionality of narrative. My Aunt Hattie would start by saying something like, "So you got the arthritis in your elbow, do you?" And then she'd say, "I got just the thing for you. You got raisins in the house? Have you got some gin that you could put the raisins in?" And that would remind her of something, which would remind her of something, and then in the center of all of this was something very contemplative. "An old lady like me, a lot of people don't listen to me, and yet I got something to tell you. You know I do."

The whole thing was singing, a very high form of poetry. That little island was a pure poem.

It's no surprise, then, that I am a writer always influenced above all else by oral storytelling and, specifically, by the American wisdom tradition in which a storyteller like Washington Irving or Mark Twain or Zora Neale Hurston or James Baldwin or Toni Morrison offers a rhythmic voice that pulls the reader past the perceived need for telling and toward the unexpected desire for enthrallment.

I'm led by voice in the same way that other writers are led by point of view or theme or plot.

Oral stories may appear conventional; their sophistication does not announce itself. They often take the form of folk tales or morality tales. They come to us through generations of storytelling and seem to take the form of tribute to old traditions. The language of these stories seems familiar. But oral stories can be seen as experimental. The relationship between storyteller and audience is often a contentious relationship in which the traditions are resisted by the audience for generational reasons; this audience, which eventually becomes the storyteller, often subverts the story and its literal meaning. Oral stories are shaped by a sense of open-ended audience/storyteller interaction (the audience present, listening, reacting); the text is, in the way we speak of experimental texts, "unfixed," interactive, an argument between shape and shapelessness.

Ensorcelled by the song of the common yellowthroat

Because I place my first trust as storyteller in the human voice, I have studied it in order to feel my way into being a better listener. Through four decades of this effort I have learned most by observing the habits of presence practiced by people with long life experience. In the voice of an elderly person we hear the many, many streams of speech (the "prior texts") that have poured into the person's own speech over a long span of time. An old voice has more moments of emptiness that are full; it has more moments of fullness struck through with emptiness.

As I've explored the dimensions of the human voice, I have

tried to learn more through study of the examples of literature, drama, music, dance; and through amateur study of the fields of rhetoric, linguistics, speech discourse, philosophy, social science, ethnomethodology, folklore, feminist theory, speech disorders, artificial intelligence, many other fields—and ornithology.

I believe it is a good habit for writers to re-conceive our own methods by picking up the tools of other trades, particularly the ones that cause us new vulnerability and openness at our workbenches.

Here is the *song* of the common yellowthroat: Wee-ter, wee-chertee, wee-chertee, wee—wee-ter, weė-chertee, wee-chertee, wee!

And here is the *call* of the common yellowthroat: Tchet. Tchet.

When we listen to the common yellowthroat singing, we hear how it casts a spell, places us in the dream-like condition; it is fulfilling because it offers fullness; it is the part of communication that is, first and foremost, transforming, though it is also transacting.

Swiftly passing experiences that endure in memory (somatic and/or cerebral memory) are often dreamlike; quite often, in such experiences a recognizable plot (action or event involving conflict that reveals causality, meaning, motivation, etc.) is merely incidental; for example: an elderly protagonist remembers rime ice on the windows of a school bus she rode as a very young child; she remembers the sound of the windshield wipers on the bus's front window; she remembers the morning light illuminating the ice; and she remembers fragmentary observations of the spellbinding, only vaguely recognizable world passing outside her window; and she remembers the smells and sounds and sights of the children around her who seemed spellbound, and she remembers the touch of the child sitting next to her who seemed spellbound and spellbinding;

at the end, and only incidentally, the reader learns that the child's father, now the senile companion of the old protagonist, was the driver of that school bus for forty years, and the reader learns that the child next to her was her sister, long estranged from her.

Anaïs Nin calls this condition of being under the spell of the present moment the experience of being "ensorcelled," a word that clearly has its root in the words for sorcery.

No dialogue, ever, between us

Singing is destabilizing since it offers us more than what we need. When we hear singing in the human voice, we recognize that the person is sound-thinking; that is, following the sound of her thoughts to the next sound. When we hear human speech that moves well beyond saying and, at length, moves further into singing, we feel how the singer is moving inward all the while she is so outwardly expressive.

It is astounding how many selves we have! And in even the most momentary singing aspects of our speech we are, as part of our true, radically generous nature, exposing our most secret selves to the world around us. "What's that?" I ask you about the faint music on the radio. If you say, "It's like a tree making that sound—that giving-way just before breaking—it's like—or not—or it is it is like dry leaves rattling everywhere and that sound of it all of it—hurting," well, you haven't answered my question, have you? You *have* made me feel something about the music of that person on the radio, Billie Holiday, and, possibly about all music, and, possibly, about radios. You have made me feel what I did not feel before, and you have given me a glimpse into *you*—your multiple selves. I might not have had that view of your very ways of being if you had not *sung* to me. Wee-ter, wee-chertee, wee-chertee, wee.

When we listen to the common yellowthroat *calling*, we hear how it wakes us up, defines terms of engagement: my turf—tchet—my nest—tchet—my neck of the woods—tchet—tchet. That "tchet" is compelling because it offers resounding completeness; it is the part of communication that is, first and foremost, transacting, though it is also transforming. It is stabilizing because it offers us just enough, just enough of what we need. When we hear calling in the human voice, we recognize that the person is think-sounding; that is, following the sound of her thoughts to the next thought. "What's that?" I ask you about the faint music on the radio. If you say, "Holiday. Billie Holiday," well, you have answered my question clearly and concisely, your tone has given the words expressiveness, and you have intensified my thought. You have given me insight into one dimension of you and into many dimensions of our terms of engagement. I would not have had that insight had you not *called* to me. Tchet. Tchet.

We humans are, after all, like birds in our vocalizations.

In this marvelous world of song and call, we hear the spectacles and dramas inherent in all trialogue and polylogue. We are reminded there is never, really, something we can accurately call dialogue. A third force and a fourth and a fifth is always present, since we cannot avoid speaking with a voice that is made up of multiple voices, and since none of us ever addresses only one other person. We are unavoidably self-addressing in any circumstance in which we seem to be addressing. I sing, "Brette! Brette! It's good to see you, Brette." But without saying it openly, I am also *asking* the Brette who knows me so well and loathes me, the old friend Brette who was a loving friend for so many years: "Brette, are you happy to see me?" And deep inside me, I'm singing to the Mc McIlvoy who sees her now, What have you done, Mc? Why did you ever ask her that?

These are spectacles, very large dramas.

And I have repeated her name, you notice—I'm singing her name—for me. And I'm singing it for Brette, too. It is good to hear someone sing your own name to you. And I'm singing her name for all of the people Brette and I mutually know who are not here, but who implicitly join our company whenever Brette and I are in each other's company.

These are dramas, intensifications of ordinary experience.

There is no dialogue between us.

Only listen

From the first rising inflection to the last falling inflection, in its coherent and incoherent elements, in its large patterns and in its particle-level constructions, our speech creates a polylogue. Our speech dynamically crowds the stage of our lives. We read a single line of speech in James Baldwin's "Sonny's Blues" or *Giovanni's Room*, and we are newly sensitized to the wonder of the inverse proportion; that is, how the infinite can be found in the infinitesimal. We hear more keenly the chord of the world in someone only singing, "It's good to see you," and calling, "Brette!" and sing-calling "Brette! Brette! It's good to see you, Brette!" It's all there: the drama of sound-thinking, the drama of think-sounding. Storytellers who are really capable of giving these subtle dramas their due must always take care not to overestimate the value of spectacles (the time-honored conventions of capital-D Dramas) found in so many conventional constructions of plot and theme.

A single word can shift all the terms of polylogue. We alter the very tone of another person's voice with a shift in our own tone. If you say, "I can't believe you made us listen to the common yellowthroat and"—and your friend interrupts to say, "*asked* us—*asked* us to listen" and you say, "Tchet!" and your friend laughs and says, "No tchet!", a revealing interaction has occurred in which the paradoxes of your relationship are now more apparent. The shift achieved by the lever of "asked" is subtle. Despite our minds and bodies constantly being pulled away from the habits of presence, our hearts are always ready to hear this kind of shift. Singing storytellers pull us away from the deafening distractions in our lives, and they ask us, "Only listen."

Your friend did not correct your opinion that I *made* you listen. With only the word "asked" your friend rekeyed your expression: same music, different key. Trying to imitate my tone of voice, you said, "Tchet!" and that rekeyed the tone of the conversation to my tone. Part of the reason you imitated my tone was to mock my rather academic tone, my male-bird tone. Your friend joined you in that mockery. You have both engaged in a regular part of human speech, which is the borrowing (not always mocking—sometimes quite affectionately mimicking) of someone else's speech. You have engaged in a kind of sound-thinking called "ventriloquation." In this ventriloquation, you have communicated to each other your attitude toward my presumptions of gender (my gender-lect), and of class and culture (my socio-lect). And now, you and your friend are in a different power/solidarity relation than you were just seventeen words earlier.

How did that happen? In the smallest dramas nested within the drama of your speech, you found what is called "acoustic rapport" and is sometimes called "rhythmic synchrony." In those smallest dramas you claimed power and gave power over; you renegotiated the solidarity between you and found new solidarity. When we listen closely to it, how can we feel anything but amazement at the outcomes of our singing and calling?

As a storyteller I find the familial context so infinitely perfect for studying the complexities of the human voice: its silences, its forms of acoustic rapport, its ventriloquations and rekeyings, its gender-lects and socio-lects, its sound-thinkings and think-soundings, its song and call.

Some moments in human speech are very naturally moments of *pouring*. We have a sense that a containing occasion and a containing relation shape that speech. The discourse of a worker to a boss, of a student to a teacher is reflective of a set of constraints. The power differential between boss and worker dictates, for the most part, that at work, in communication about tasks, the boss will do most of the singing and most of the calling. Granting that there are exceptions to the rule, that same power differential means that the worker's speech is mostly constative, language expressing what is. The boss's speech is both constative and performative. The boss's language is performative because it can perform things, it can make things happen. The boss's speech is referred to as "high involvement" speech (demanding attention) and the worker's speech is "high consideration" speech (demanding little or no attention).

Some moments in human speech are very naturally moments of *spilling*. We have a sense that a releasing occasion and a releasing relation shape that speech, as in the discourse of a client to a therapist and the discourse of college roommates. The speech for the roommates will be both constative and performative, though to varying degrees. Both people can make things happen in their speech; both can expect high involvement and high consideration. In the context of our families and the family-like intimate groups that we are a part of, there is every imaginable kind of pouring and spilling.

In the company of our family members, a person will move freely from pouring out what "I" feel to spilling out what "we" feel to spilling and pouring out what one faction of "we" feel about another faction of "they." It is perfectly natural for me to lie to my biscuit-baking cousin: "I don't care what they say, we like your biscuits—I mean that, we all really do." In the context of family, the first-person voice and the first-person-plural voice move freely back and forth as part of a process of revealing the Selves, the Self, and the True Self. We keenly perceive our ways of being and our ways of becoming in the unique pourings and spillings of familial interaction.

Whether in a coherent family or a chaotic family, the pouring and spilling will not be held back, the indignities of exposure will not be postponed. Through these pourings and spillings, our various masks must come off, one at a time; our own most persistent central delusion must dissolve; our secret nature must emerge: the inevitability of these educing developments is the very stuff of storytelling.

The white open spaces

Related to the phenomenon of acoustic rapport is the matter of silence, since there is rhythm and broken rhythm in the expressive ways silence marks our speech.

Human beings' first language is silence. You may know someone who is a really silent person; someone who has remained not just coherent in their silence but expressive in it. For most people, what falls away is their first language, silence. But when you speak that language, when you are "abnormal" enough that it has remained your first language, you hear the world in a different way.

My use of white space is expressive silence—lots of it. It enacts spilling more than pouring. It creates sonic shifts in the associative mode rather than the dramatic mode.

I examine the white spaces I find in my drafts to remind myself that my shared experience with the character was *incomplete*, though I may have thought it was complete.

In those white spaces, I can intuit what I do *not* know about the characters—what the narrator of the work cannot articulate, for instance, about his or her motivations. I am especially interested in narrators who come right up against knowing but still do *not* know their own motivations, or untrustworthy narrators who stop right at the point of revealing or acknowledging their motivations.

These unknowable, inexpressible parts of the text often present *good doubt*—a reminder that a unique narrative voice is defined as much by what is *not* said as by what *is* said. When we're rereading our story drafts we must, of course, pay attention to the white spaces that are just *bad debt*—a place of self-censorship, for instance—that should be paid off, but we should pay attention too to the places of good doubt.

The white spaces in our drafts give evidence of what the writer has erased: big chunks of exposition, authorial intrusion into a narrator's voice, minor characters who pushed their way into the work and were booted out, whole substories that insinuated themselves (perhaps wanting to *be* the story), extended scenes with expository dialogue, or, in a late draft, perhaps after great resistance and suffering, the excision of the image, idea, bit of scene or dialogue that was the starting place, the *donnée,* because it is now completely irrelevant to what the work has become.

In the white spaces in my drafts, I can see what risks I took by erasing text and what risks I avoided. How do you make these space decisions in your work? When do you make most of them? In composing? In revising? More in your early drafts than in your final drafts? What do they mean?

You could ask yourself what might go where the space is. Setting? Passing of time? The character at last alone, not in scene with other characters? Suppose a section ends with a character eating an egg sandwich at 4 a.m. How does the room look? What does 4 a.m. in winter in Roswell, New Mexico, feel like?

Perhaps the space is a place of deflation. What you expected to happen, what you expected to experience with the characters is withheld—for what purpose? Is that narrator not ready yet?

Is it possible that the story the characters want to write exists in these spaces, while you willfully write the story you meant to write?

My use of white space offers a graphic distinction from so-called "normal" presentation. It uses paragraphing as attention to tonal clusters rather than as building materials of theme, or as the foundation, the centering and the supporting walls of plot.

For example, in my novel *One Kind Favor,* there is a panel-like sense of leaping across gaps and chasms in the fifty-four sections of the novel, just as there is such a sense in twelve or eight bars of blues music, and just as there is in meandering oral narratives in which the storyteller confronts his own community with its irreal absences and presences and shameful and sacred silences.

Most of us first use white space to organize the work—to "order" the chaos. This might be a good outcome of our early learning as essayists. It might not be. We mark off beginning, middle, and end with white space, especially in drafting. Most of us put in space for a major shift in setting, or in time. We put in space to move from one narrative voice to another, from one narrative point of view to another. In a story that will go in many directions, we put in space to bring one part of the story to closure and signal a new direction—to suggest *completedness* when moving from one part of the story to another. We might be making a novel "navigable"—helping the reader move across large pods of character development, action, themes, background information, or imagery.

The problem I see in most of these "organizing" principles is that so many forms of modern narrative, especially first-person narratives but also most good third-person narratives, naturally *resist* being completed, naturally *resist* offering beginning, middle, and end. Most narrators don't know as they recollect or trace in present tense what part of their experience was the beginning, what part the middle, what part the end.

Space breaks can instead be used to suppress coherence, to disrupt and dislocate. For instance, Faulkner's *The Sound and the Fury.* The text flips back and forth in time, in perspective. The few white spaces there heighten our sense of suspended causal connections. We may want, as readers, to order the work, perhaps for the sake of controlling our own lives, but Faulkner disorders the work, complicates our lives. What did you do at the white spaces when you first read *The Sound and the Fury?* I stopped. I paged backwards and read that last section again. The white space invited me to read recursively.

We *could* organize a story by our own version of caesura. In poetics, there are three types: fading juncture—a voice falling off; rising juncture—a question implicitly or explicitly posed; and sustained juncture—a voice breaking into momentary silence without having risen or fallen perceptibly in pitch before the silence.

In my own work, I cannot separate space breaks from overall story structure. The story is organized by movements—sets of sensual, emotional experiences meant to intensify and constantly change in value. The white space is not necessarily an organizational marker; it is often a silence with a certain value.

The silences are there to help the reader get through the incoherence.

They show us how to *speak* the text, *perform* it, *sing* it—how to fade out and fade in from one voice to another—and they remind us: this text is not to be only *received.*

The centrifugal human voice

It is only human for our spilling voice to become, sometimes, our nonsense-making voice: the voice that momentarily undoes the meaning it or another voice has offered. You've been witness, I'm sure, to the moment when conversation is on track, everyone is talking about the same topic, feeding into the same levels of think-sounding and sound-thinking, and this harmony is interrupted by someone's completely unrelated chaotic spilling out of Too Much Information. It punctures the moment, makes nonsense of our careful sense-making. In our responses to it, new dimensions of our character are revealed. When these moments are most horrifying is when they are most readily suited to comedy; Mark Twain and Eudora Welty captured these moments splendidly.

I strongly believe that one of the primary pleasures in life—certainly one of the comic pleasures—is to see our world fall out of shape, to witness within the world of the work deteriorating and destabilizing moments that *never* again reach a stable, generative state.

Grace Paley, one of my personal heroes, whom I believe is one of the best writers in the comic mode *ever*, will put three characters together in the briefest story, and something about that dynamic of three will feel inherently chaotic in its marvelous energy. Her stories are "experimental" in their treatment of scene and dialogue, but also in their narrative skid. They skid from one thing to another in such a way that you either have to learn in the first sentences what that experience is going to be and commit to it, or you pretty swiftly say, "No, thanks." Another such writer is Stanley Elkin. Every moment is in flux—about to become something else; something else is about to emerge from it, something else behind it is about to become apparent.

Out of spilling and pouring speech, out of the many forms of silence, out of the crowded stage of our polylogues, what sometimes arrives with terrifying, exhilarating force in a voice is simply a crying out. It is a moment in speech that is more spontaneous than all other moments. In certain cases, it takes the form of a long, long rant or a directionless, extended self-emptying of grief or love or fear or ecstasy. In certain instances, it is a single word or phrase. I have read that the poet Dylan Thomas said he began each writing session by putting down the one letter, "O," because of his assumption that all poetry begins and ends there.

The human cry is always present, if we will hear it. Our era has put it into the air in a great chaos of song and call coming from all edges of the world. Some of it is centripetal languaging, finding a center, a point. Some of it is centrifugal languaging, moving outward and outward.

When it is orderly, coherent, centripetal—"I had a job once"—the human cry, the compounded expression of joy and grief, of anchoring memory and lostness, is easy to hear only in passing. "I had a job once! I had a job once. Once, I had a job": only five words, after all, easy for the listener to forget, easy to dismiss.

When it is chaotic, incoherent, inarticulate, centrifugal—"It was, I had, my hands could, my hands would, my arms, people knew once I could, they knew, they knew, I was my job, I mean, I mean..."—when it comes to us in this form, the human cry causes us dynamic agitation with its ambivalence, its elusiveness, its wildness. We find ourselves *wishing* to but utterly unable to forget that crying-out, to dismiss it. Such cries occur in the fiction of Zora Neale Hurston, John Steinbeck, and Toni Morrison. As I read their works I move past mastering ways of knowing; I am learning to *feel* what I know about the human voice.

That very pretty apron is motive enough

We read the words, "It is said..." and we already sense, in sadness, the future, "...from that day to this, Frog and Snake have never played together again." We hear the words, "People say..." and we feel in our bodies the outcome, "...and The Black Grouper vowed never to fall in love with a human girl again." At the words, "There once was..." we already wish for and fear the failure of all adult self-understanding and all adult instruction realized in the story's last words, "...and never again opened the door."

The teller in the Grimm stories lowers the bucket of her voice into the well of the reader's gut through the hypnosis and auto-hypnosis of the words "once upon a time." She (scholars conjecture that women storytellers were the main source for the Grimm brothers' fairy tales) understands that the about-to-be moment for her audience is like the dream and reverie threshold states in which we are *upon* time, not before or past it. We are in Child Time.

And children, so corruptible in their innocence, so irrevocably vulnerable, are always at the threshold of the dream and reverie states. (No wonder we associate these folk tales with bedtime tales.) We—the children all adult and all so-called children's stories are written for—are helpless against the past time, the past perfect progressive what-had-been time; and we wish for the passive future perfect continuous, the what-will-have-been time—but...but...we are in a story, we are upon time.

The Upon Time is a gift the reader desires beyond her or his understanding.

The reader is always a child. And that child is always making a wish. To be a reader is to be a wisher willing the next moment into being.

The writer trying to inhabit the moment the reader inhabits understands that the first moment of the reading experience, the about-to-be moment is, after all, The Wishing Moment, whether it is the moment the narrator wishes to make a curse or wishes to bless, or whether she makes a wish only because her mouth opened and out came the hidden desire (the frog-like, snake-like, grouper-like desire swimming, slithering, croaking) that makes a story the moment it is exhaled. No tale exists, after all, if desire is left unsaid.

We readers join the narrator in The Wishing Moment. We know it is time for this moment because the words "once upon a time" have been invoked. Notice that no overly self-conscious writer is second-guessing those four words, which are recapitulated in the oral tradition of almost every culture in the world.

This imminence is a part of the early language listening experiences that never disappear from the later reading experiences. In recollecting the power of Italian folk tales and fairy tales on his development as an artist, Italo Calvino stresses how much he learned from the "delaying, cyclic, motionless" quality of narrative time in them.

Neither at the beginning nor at the tale's end does the teller imagine anything but a reader in a state of fully engaged *delight* in the terrible initiations, the dismemberments, the violations, the cruel punishments, the deceptions, the exposures, the mercies, the tendernesses, the re-memberments, and the satisfying vengeances that follow that greeting, "Once upon a time."

The teller of the Grimm story finds the wish-bewitchments of peasants and the bitch-bewishments of royalty all part of the same childlike wonder. The teller imagines a highly suggestible audience in the figurative and literal dark, in a place of no persisting light, in a condition of poverty or great wealth, in lostness or confusion or doom, and in most cases, *marked* by their condition. In other words, the teller imagines an audience sharing much in common with the folk tale's characters marked by the caul, by the crooked chin, by the crutches on which they hobble. These characters are not really what we in our supreme creative writing court robes would readily call "characters," since instead of faces they have roles: the roles of kings, queens, of tailors, of spinsters, of servant girls, of fisherman, fishermen's wives, thieves, thumblings, poor mothers, stepmothers, poor daughters, robbers, robbers' sons, soldiers (many soldiers in the Grimm stories, soldiers just after war, and having no money and no skills but soldiering skills). They have problems: the problem of surviving, the problem of abandonment, of needing to escape the Evil One—and, in the case of the royal characters, the problem of succession. They are marked. They have roles. They have problems. They are familiar but they are in the faceless-about-to-have-face condition.

Why does the audience for the Grimm tales care about them? The audience is invested in them because of making wishes for them to be miserable in countless ways, because of willing them to have countless paths out of—or much, much deeper into—their misery. This is a corrupt and corruptible, not a pure and redeemable reader the teller is imagining. This is an irrecoverable reader the teller will not presume to recover, to save. Baudelaire imagined this same reader. In our era, Angela Carter and Russell Edson and Yusunaro Kawabata have imagined this reader. How inviolate a reader, I wonder, was E.B. White writing for in that opening passage of *Charlotte's Web*: "Where is Papa goin' with that ax?"

At the same moment we readers are adjusting to the uncertainties of Upon Time—at that same moment the Grimm tales give us an opportunity to learn presence—they distract us with the threat of the future. At every turn that the tales impart or enact virtue they subvert it or explode it; it is an understandable but unfortunate misreading of the Grimm tales that they are morality tales; they are oral tales coming from an "I" teller with no real sense of ownership since the tale arises from the "we" of the tribe, of the community, of the fellowship in a group that is unstable: violent, full of thieves and witches, of devolving mysterious contracts between the natural and the human world. These plural first-person narrators are the embodiment of the permeable child psyche in which the I/mother, I/family, I/dog, I/doll, I/friend are so irreducibly the same—I *am* my doll; I *am* my scary, marvelous mother who intentionally cuts herself; and I *am* my marvelous, exuberant friend who has given first and last names to her lips and teeth. And because I *am* multitudes (thank you Buddha, thank you Whitman, thank you Artist Formerly Known as Prince)—because I am multitudes, if my "fair and good" stepsister, who I *am*, has a "very pretty apron" ("Roland"), she *should* die, she deserves to die by having her head cut off when she is asleep. That very pretty apron is motive enough.

It freaks out really adult adults. Those adult adults are not our readers, dear poets and fiction writers. I say give the adult adults what they ask for: bad nonfiction. If you *want* them freaked (an honorable goal), give them nonfiction with the unbounded mind of great poems and stories in which the about-to-be moment is *not* a "teachable moment."

Imminence first, imminence last

We should not write The Teachable. And we should revise in such a way that we scrutinize the value of The Teachable. That is the wisdom of the Grimm tales.

They are re-told and re-told and re-told tales. The best of the retellings constitute processes of revision in which most or all of original intent is lost, perhaps *forever*. And what accumulates is wonder.

Sherwood Anderson's first-person story, "Death in the Woods," is a re-told story. The narrator's brother has told it to their mother and sister. Restless with *how* his brother told it, the narrator retells the story of Mrs. Grimes's death in the woods. There is no clear "point" to the story: she is a figure who can be contemplated but not comprehended. We are told the could-be, might-be mystery of her *impels* the narrator.

The narrator has been impelled and agitated by Mrs. Grimes's life, the unanswerable substructures (the smallest and most enigmatic cohesive elements) of it; he has not been compelled and calmed by the reasons for her death, the superstructures (the big timbers of plot, symbology, etc.). Meaning does not accumulate in the retellings—magic does, and magic has the effect of undoing clarity regarding cause and effect, of disrupting logical plot progression.

The story will be unsatisfying to us if it does not carry us past and again into another and another and another about-to-be-mystery. A good tale offers imminence first, imminence last. The hero cannot yet *become*. He must *be*. We, then, experience the kind of immediacy that makes us feel more and more sensitive to our experiences *upon* time. The tale suspends the experiences of the body and mind and invites the reader to feel the strange goodness of that suspension.

"The Shoes Which Were Danced to Pieces" is a good example of a tale that ends on imminence. To summarize it simply: some people dance their shoes to pieces, all their shoes; the oldest and most experienced dancers ignore the youngest; people lose their heads in their earnest tasks, and the survivors, so we are told, "were again bewitched in as many days as they had danced."

And here is the final part of "A Tale of One Who Traveled to Learn What Shivering Meant":

> Then the King said, "You have won the castle, and shall marry my daughter."
>
> "This is all very fine," replied the youth, "but still I don't know what shivering means."
>
> So the gold was fetched, and the wedding was celebrated, but the young Prince (for the youth was a Prince now), notwithstanding his love for his bride, and his great contentment, was still continually crying, "If I could but shiver! If I could but shiver!" At last it fell out in this wise: one of the chambermaids said to the Princess, "Let me bring in my aid to teach him what shivering is." So she went to the brook which flowed through the garden, and drew up a pail of water full of little fish; and, at night, when the young Prince was asleep, his bride drew away the covering and poured the pail of cold water and the little fish over him, so that they slipped all about him. Then the Prince woke up directly, calling out, "Oh! That makes me shiver! Dear wife, that makes me shiver! Yes, now I know what shivering means!"

What is the teachable moment here?

This? Reader, in the end you will still want what you can't have, including the weird thing you can't have.

This? Reader, you will at last marry, and your love for and contentment with your bride will leave you wanting the weird thing.

Or? Reader, you will have a husband wanting the weird thing. It is best to have a chambermaid more perverse than you. It is good to have a pail.

Or? Reader, it is not the cold water you throw on the one you love that matters. It is the little fishes. Remember to put the little fishes in, with their scales and sharp fins.

There is no teachable moment here. Here is a new imminence, a new about-to-be moment.

The writer who hurries us past the imminent moment mistakenly assumes the reader wants to quickly be done with the hypnotic sense of ending inside beginning. The result of this hurrying is that both beginning and ending are unsatisfying or only satiating. (It is possible that what most often causes Writer's Block is what causes Reader's Block: impatience with imminence.)

If as we write, we assume the reader wishes to experience the story or poem in this childlike about-to-be dream state (including the states of reverie, the states of unimpeded, uncensored euphoria, the states of persisting and deforming anxiety, the states of abiding, emptying calm), we more readily set aside our assumptions about stabilizing the first moments of the reading experience.

The child reader is the nest holding the adolescent and adult reader; it's not the other way around. Do not fail the childlike, innocent reader, writers. Do not fail to be childlike and innocent yourself as you write.

Witnessing the drama of present experience perishing, regard the enigmas of eternity.

Witnessing the ineffable in the experience of time and space, evoke presence mindfully.

I grew up in a curious mixture of Catholicism, first in a town called Madison, Illinois. My mother's family had emigrated from Lithuania, and our church was part of a Polish community that rarely spoke English. While the mass was in Latin, the singing was always inflected with the Polish dialect. I memorized all the Latin because I served as an altar boy. No one, even for a moment, thought to teach altar boys what the Latin meant. And people attending the mass could not translate that Latin. Their first language was Polish, they were struggling to learn English, and they were there for a mass in Latin. And yet it worked very like the way pre-language works—when you hear an infant first verging into language and they mutter something that is not language at all, but you know exactly what they mean. That pre-language reminds you that the way in which language works first in the world is to cast a spell. "I want that water. If I make this sound, you will give me that water." Is that not magic? Is that not mysticism?

When we moved to Granite City, we belonged to a church that was dominated by Irish Roman Catholics—specifically, the Franciscans. The Franciscans have a deep sense of mysticism inherited from Saint Francis, who it is said could speak to the birds and to the animals, who spoke back to him. This was always part of his conversation with God. By that time, the mass was no longer in Latin, and many people in that church resented deeply that it was not. They wanted Latin back. They wanted a service, a sacred occasion in which they both would understand and would have no understanding at all, which many people say is the very root of mysticism.

Trenchant, riddling, unresolved experiences—paradox—have value independent of ever being solved.

Preserving fullness of lostness

The "object in its veil" wrote Walter Benjamin, "becomes the idea of the impossibility of unveiling."

A storyteller can evoke the horror appearing from under the holy veils of experience, the holiness emerging from under the veils of horror. In James Baldwin's *Giovanni's Room*, at its imminent moment and in its desinent moment, there are veils upon veils. In this way, the story, passing and sublime, acknowledges the fullness of opposing impulses: the sense of sadness about the ending of one manifestation of self; the sense of exhilaration about the passing. The author has chosen two particular moments in the work to intensify the reader's sense of what is "not representable" (the unnameable, beyond expression). In making this choice, the writer undermines the reader's sense of what is "presentable" (nameable, expressible).

Giovanni's Room begins with the narrator's rambling—he is drinking and determined to be drunk by morning—about where he is, a house in the south of France, about his own reflection, about the train he will be taking to Paris, and more then, about this house, followed by over five hundred words of wandering memory about his fiancée Hella, about how untrustworthy he is in his reckoning with his own story. He ends this imminent passage with, "If this were not so I would not be alone in this house tonight. Hella would not be on the high seas. And Giovanni would not be about to perish, sometime between this night and this morning, on the guillotine."

In the desinent moment before the book's ending David/ Giovanni scene, there is an extended scene between David and Hella. In this scene, Hella guides them toward a discussion of how women are at the mercy of men, and David insists that men are at the mercy of women, and they arrive at no agreement, and, actually, in this effort at dialogue they utterly confuse each other about their individual true selves and about the truths of their relationship. They run into Jacques, an important antagonist in the work; he remarks about how David has been hiding from his friends, has abandoned his "baby" Giovanni; the implication of the encounter is that David has been false to everyone and is unrecognizable to his friends, to his fiancée, to himself. This coming-to-an-end moment dramatizes that the characters understand each other *not at all;* as for David and Hella, it emphasizes that each of them *expected* love to set things right, and that together they will likely prove to each other such an outcome has been, and is, and will be impossible.

If the imminent and desinent moments were not given their veiled power in *Giovanni's Room* the reader would find it easy to quite reductively assert, "The meaning of this work of fiction is... The purpose of this work of fiction is..." and the reader's sense of justice would readily exclude a sense of arbitrariness, accident, and error. Baldwin has invited the reader to inhabit the self that asks beauty to be powerful, sensible, and purposeful; he has, in the totality of the reading experience, also invited the reader to put that self aside, to ask beauty to be power-relenting, insensible, and purposeless.

The David/Hella scene I've referenced offers the kind of awareness that one feels in nature where three stages of lostness easily occur: the sensual flooding that makes us feel oddly disinterested in direction—even if we have a map in our hands and a clear trail before us; the experience of dreamtime so immediate that our cognitive orientation to temporal source is replaced by somatic orientation to temporal echo; and the dissolution of individuality that elementally changes the "I to myself" conversation and that heightens the sense of singularity while it burns the very wick of it down. A work of literature, like *Giovanni's Room*, that unveils *and* veils, that paradoxically offers a sense of form preserving fullness of lostness: that is what I'll call a masterpiece.

Please note that I am not arguing at all for a kind of veiling that merely obscures everything for the reader, causing the reader frustration. If veiling the moment, then veil it for the sake of tension, suspense, and altered apprehension, not to invite confusion, vagueness, and unfair terms of engagement.

I am arguing for causing the reader *regret*: the sense of leave-taking regret experienced as the inevitabilities that cause the definite sense of an end; regret to be leaving the illusions of pleasure, to be leaving the illusions of suffering.

Our lives are richer for such moments of regret that change the very ground of our condition; our literature is naturally richer if we will give such moments their due.

The incarnate condition

Twenty-first century American realism has so dedicated itself to avoiding condemnation as "touchy feely" that our work too often merely says instead of sings, articulates instead of expresses. We American writers lean on false assumptions that there is only, after all, one legitimate mode because there is only one dominant mode.

We have been so fearful of the touchy feely effects for so long that now our stories are always, always and finally, more thought than felt. We no longer know how to make readers actually *feel* physical revulsion about torture and the isolation of prison, and we no longer know how to make readers *feel* contempt in their very flesh for those who want us to devalue same-sex love and those who ask us to ignore our fierce *physical* loyalty to the earth's body.

A felt response to language, what *it enacts* and not just what *it imparts*—a radical commitment to somatic force—marks the sensibility of Fyodor Dostoevsky, Virginia Woolf, Vladimir Nabokov, D.H. Lawrence, Franz Kafka, Henry Miller, Gertrude Stein, and Anaïs Nin. Nin's thirty-five thousand pages of journals were truly extraordinary efforts to present the "physical climate" of living in her body, of being fully present to that "furnace of affections, loves, desires...reveries." "I only believe in fire," she wrote, and added that her writing efforts offered "the story of my incendiary neurosis."

Nin readily frustrates the reader who might expect her work to be at the service of the balanced forms of realism, and who will not respect the absolute realism there that speaks to the child in the adult reader. André Breton wrote in his 1924 manifesto of surrealism that "at an early age children are weaned on the marvelous, and later on they fail to retain a sufficient virginity of mind to thoroughly enjoy fairy tales....There are fairy tales to be written for adults, fairy tales still almost blue."

I believe Nin wrote so well about the body because she invested her work with that fairy-tale, mythic quality in which characters absolutely fix their attention on the present moment, on what they *feel*—the "something there" that is unnameable—Whitman called it "prehension"—not on what they will be able—in three seconds, hours, days—to identify.

Those of us trying to make touchy feely fairy tales that just might—might—decenter the reader could read Anaïs Nin's work in order to learn in our own work how to acknowledge more often the possibilities of the marvelous; how to more often concede the primacy of *thought* story elements to *felt* story elements; how to recognize whether we have ineffectively presented an inherently destabilizing environment as stabilizing; how to fully honor the character's physical sensations while exploring the possibilities of prehension, of that "something there" feeling; how to present surrogate pain and pleasure; and how to generously give the sense of what charged objects the character encounters in the labyrinths of ingression.

More sex

As an editor and teacher I have written this request in my comments on manuscripts. I have written, "Why not more sex?" in the margins of manuscripts, and I have also written, "Should the pace be *slower* here?"

In certain instances in which narration has summarized sexual interaction between characters or in which asterisks have left that interaction to the imagination, I have written, "Consider actually presenting the sex scene here."

More Good Sex is what I would like us to consider as writers. What I mean by "Good Sex" is that the sexual interactions between characters deepen the mystery of them and confirm their complexity without ever inviting the reader to say, "This sexual behavior equals this unarguable assumption about the character."

"Good Sex" should intensify the relationship between the reader and the characters. Perhaps the reader feels the story has shifted into a reader/character intimacy that is suddenly more complicated and is somehow unsettling. Good. Perhaps the reader feels momentarily alienated by the sexual interactions of the characters; if this alienation (what has been called an "estrangement effect") increases tensions between the reader and character in compelling ways, then good. What is deadlier than a character who behaves as the reader thinks the character *should*?

Depending on the narrative perspective I am writing in, almost *any* interaction, almost any behavior is potentially sexual. I believe the pornographic writer does not ever quite learn this lesson and, so, exclusively portrays all sexual interaction as genital. I recommend making the Hindu text on physical and spiritual love, the *Kama Sutra*, part of your writer's library, right next to the dictionary. A typical passage says that on the ninth hour of the ninth day together the man should hold the woman's foot in his lap and warm it with his hands and press his thumb between her toes and sing to her without looking into her eyes. The woman, who should keep her eyes open and watching, should hold a betel leaf, a stimulant, in her mouth.

Writers who are experienced students of the body and of copulation should be careful not to replace drama with spectacle in their work.

The writer should not assume dialogue is important in the sex scene. Nonverbal communication can establish immediate intimacy between characters.

The writer should commit to each moment of the narrator's obsessions, not editing whatever passages put the reader at risk of intimacy but, in fact, editing whatever passages leave the reader *safe* and the reader's experience unvaried.

The writer's first purpose is not brevity. The writer should encourage some tension between the reader and the narrator.

The writer should invite into the narration those moments of impingement that are characteristic of intimacy. By "impingement" I mean the way the parts of one sentence act upon another, impinge on each other in odd ways that have nothing to do with logic and everything to do with the mysteries of human nature.

In becoming students of the body's mysteries we might become real students of eros, not reducing eros to sex, not deconstructing love in our storytelling but reconstructing it.

Once, in my homework for a novel, I visited a farm where a family had lived for three generations. Having met the couple then living there, and having explained that I was a storyteller widely known nowhere, and having asked if I could imaginatively "lease" their 220 acres for one chapter, they walked me to their family burial ground, told me about their living children, told me about their twins, who died at the ages of five and six. The woman said, "I can't talk about it," and the man said, "No, we can't," and the woman said, "But I wanted you to see."

I have trained myself to recognize truths in people's manner of speech and in their physical movements. Nothing could have been more intimate than that brief visit to the graves of their twins. Already—and this is an embarrassing confession—I was mentally fictionalizing this couple and their relationship. When the narrative I planned to write leaves the graveyard it would be the right time for a sex scene between them. It would be the right time for me to choose the drama of their lovemaking—the narrator fully imagining their lovemaking—over the spectacle of remaining too long at the graveyard.

Am I wrong in thinking that more graveyard observation and dialogue would be "gratuitous" while the imagined sex scene would sustain and maybe intensify the reader's intimacy with them and the narrator? In my reading experience and, I admit, my writing experience, it seems to me sentimentality is more often gratuitous in our storytelling than sexuality.

God The Uppercase, god the lower

I wish to succeed in communicating my respect for all of us as true believers—in beauty: in its life-transforming silences and absences, its face in the whirlwind and its face reflected in stillness, its force in the forms of chaos and coherence, its direct experiences of embodied and intellectual engagement, its inherent dualities in regard to whether beauty must have use in the world, as if a robot—or must not, as if a rhododendron.

I assume that writers' convictions about the importance of beauty are "religious." I assume that our personal sense of mission could be fairly characterized as "zealous." I assume that in our singular dedication to the cathedral of a story we have felt so physically dislocated, so psychically transported, so utterly fixated about the smallest details of ceremony and the most arcane articles of temple construction that we agree we could be described as "fanatic." I assume that as readers and as artists many of us have already experienced—or are actively, quite irrationally welcoming—more than one powerful "conversion" experience in our sensibilities, and that in that rebirth we would accept being named "born again."

I assume that our utter failures as artists have often been more significant in our development than our successes, so much so that sometimes those failures have felt less like setbacks in the life of The Artist than like "sins" against The Art. I assume that when our work bends slightly or turns radically away from our intentions, we begin to confront our unanswerable and unnameable incarnate prehensions. We often helplessly call these prehensions of beauty "mystical" and barely restrain ourselves from using other words arriving in our minds: "divine," "holy," "spiritual."

We can identify, then, with writers who have consciously shaped their works—and, in some cases, had their works disfigured—according to absolute assumptions about moral instruction in art. We are readers of Hawthorne, Hurston, Baldwin, Steinbeck, and O'Connor, of Cervantes, Hugo, Mann, Dickens, and Kafka—and, so, we have met God, masked and unmasked, in God's many manifestations in countless modes of fiction. When we have most wanted the members of our congregation of readers and writers to feel awe about the soul's splendors and its evils, we have read the Russian novelists for whom the temptations of power, sensuality, and hypocrisy are never examined exclusive of God as a signifying presence or absence.

I believe storytellers must think imaginatively about God as a tension-causing character, certainly more imaginatively than history and sometimes philosophy have thought. We may need to think more *innocently* about God than theology and organized religion have or ever will. If we find ourselves leaving God out of our pages in which God is directly relevant to the characters' ways of being and becoming, is it because we novelists and short story writers lack the capacity to think innocently?

Tolstoy, for example, in *Master and Man*, does not wish to teach through the artistic mechanism of irony but through a kind of reverent sincerity. It is a story coming from a writer who always—in every work, early and late—wished to teach but wished to exercise mystical intuition in arriving at the story's instructive revelations. It does not wish to teach and *comfort*, and, so, while it invites the concentrated ardor of faith as a response, it does not narrow readers to feeling what Simone Weil would call "the smugness of the false elect."

If *Master and Man* gave us only Brekhunoff's business arrangement with God, a negotiating relationship, and not also Nikita's consenting relationship, the imaginative transformation of God as a character would be less effective. The question of the active and the passive quality of these relationships between the character God and other characters is an important one.

A direct technique lesson from *Master and Man*: in portraying God in fiction, remember the figure of God often is accompanied by his disfigured double, god.

Tolstoy gives iconic prominence to god the Money, god the Power, god the Art, god the Church. We understand that the worship of these lowercase gods is inherently evil, and that those who commit that evil do not slowly begin to die in their souls—but, in fact, *die in their souls* and then linger so that we can gradually take in the instantaneous implications for any one character who is in conflict with the uppercase God. We see, for instance, in *Master and Man* that Brekhunoff's wife and son are both described as pale, and we can imply that by association with Brekhunoff they, too, are already dead souls. Without those serious implications, Tolstoy seems to insist, a writer would be better off only writing about the lowercase god.

As I have remembered my reading experiences in *War and Peace*, *Anna Karenina*, *Family Happiness*, *The Kreutzer Sonata*, and *The Death of Ivan Ilyich*, it seems to me no single writer I have ever read has portrayed the frozen soul—frozen by war, frozen by love denied or betrayed, frozen by hypocrisy in faith or falseness in the vows of brotherhood—better than Tolstoy. I do not admire his work more than the works of Dostoevsky and Mann and Porter in which we see the human soul in its freezing culminations, or the works of Melville and Dickens and Chekhov and Baldwin in which we witness the soul thawing, or of Faulkner and Conrad and Cather in which the soul resists either thawing or freezing. But I admire the patience with which he makes the key characters, *already dead*, compelling for the many masks they must wear, and the hypocritical ceremonies of the living they must participate in in their attempts to hide from themselves or others that fact.

One good reason for us to consciously try to write God as a major or minor character into our stories that invite such possibility is to test whether we are prepared to constructively consent to the loss of our exhaustive knowledge—God as concept (not necessarily as character) *has been written about often, after all*—in our composing or revising processes.

Let's assume that a new opportunity has arrived for growing more literary work of the merit of contemporary American writers like Toni Morrison, Walker Percy, Annie Dillard, and Charles Johnson who give presence to the compelling and curious character of God in their works.

The ways in which God *changes* as a character—God as a developing character—are important to pay attention to because once we commit to uppercase God inhabiting our fiction, we should make that choice matter.

That seems obvious, right? Not so obvious. American literary culture has, in the past, conspired to make some of us still nervous about this, and because some of that fearfulness endures, we will prefer for God to remain in the work for the single purpose of being irrelevant.

A bad choice. At the least, an unimaginative choice.

Space-time

The marvel of prehension, the "something there" sensation, is that makes it possible for us to say time and space and individual and collective reality are different than we might ever have comprehended.

My seizures until the age of nine would leave me with an acute memory of the moment just before—such as the odd intensification of something very insubstantial, perhaps light in the fold of a curtain; an acute memory of the moment of coming to; and no memory of the moment of seizure. My brothers, my cousins, my schoolmates would ask, "What is it like?" I was pretty sure they were asking about the spectacle (the seizure), not the drama (all the rest). I always had to say, "I don't know."

What is it that makes a poem of your life? It is usually a paradox. For me, it is dislocation in time. Being robbed of remembering the spectacle has caused me to live in the imminence of the past (the about-to-be moment already passing); it has caused me to live in the imminence of the future (the about-to-be moment already arriving). I am a chronomaniac because of all that. I've been trying to understand more about time since my first not-remembered seizure.

Finding language for characters who feel or struggle to feel "incarnated"; that is, in full possession of their own bodies if only for brief moments, writers must think of how our experience of space-time alters according to our characters' pains, their fears, their pleasures, their compromised pleasures, their obsessions, their dreams, and their reveries. What woman or man can we possibly write about who does not have these as their constant or, in any case, persistent companions? What woman or man can we possibly write about who is not sensitive, at least in passing, to the pain present in the beloved or estranged or estranged-beloved family member or friend?

I recommend to you Miroslav Holub's remarkable essay, "The Dimension of the Present Moment," in which he proposes that the concept of the ego in the present moment lasts three seconds. His essay echoes some of the central concepts in Alfred North

Whitehead's masterpiece of speculative philosophy, *Process and Reality* (first published in 1929); I recommend Whitehead to any writer who wishes to have all their first principles of narrative demolished, who wants to be reminded of "the buzzing world" as Descartes, Newton, Locke, Hume, and Kant tried to describe space-time existence. See also Wordsworth's "Immortality Ode" in which he contemplates the "vanishings" that a child recollects of "a condition in which it was very nearly true that he and his environment were one." And for certain concepts of sensation and somatic process, I recommend Joan Richardson's essay, "Music Is Thinking, Then, Sound," taking its title from Wallace Stevens's "Peter Quince at the Clavier."

Time stabilizes or destabilizes for the characters according to their sense of their environment changing constantly, no matter how unchanging it seems to others.

Time dilates or contracts for them according to their sense of the "in-between" states of pleasure and pain that return them to a kind of infancy, a feeling of being without words and, so, more fully inside their sensations of "something there," their prehensions—not comprehensions, but prehensions.

Time flows or breaks according to the characters' sense of what good and bad "experience parcels" (Nin's term) their bodies remember, the splinters of memory that they feel in their flesh, particularly the absences they feel in their flesh. This is related, as well, to the influence of sensitivity to others' bodies.

Time deforms and re-forms, swings as if measured by a pendulum, according to the characters' prehensions of charged objects, which may serve as triggers for other heightened physical responses or for the shutting down of physical responses.

Time is most unstable—deforming, re-forming—at "the magic hour": the moment in time at which the character is most vulnerable.

Moments in time do not suggest outward progression so much as they reflect ingression, a moving inside and deeper inside, accompanied by the senses intermingling; that is, the synesthesia in which color describes sound, scent describes touch, words embody and do not merely impart.

Space-time is relevant to revision. Our characters experience a specific space-time. The sentences we make to *construct* this space-time end up *creating* a space-time. "Where have you been?" people ask the writer. "I've been inside this story," the writer answers. After long silence, the writer answers, "I've been inside this sentence."

It might be helpful to consider three particularly dominant modes of temporal experience that scientific research suggests: *pre-perceptual categorization,* in which one experiences *prehending* (the something-there sensation) through the senses; *perceptual categorization,* in which one experiences *apprehending* through the senses; and *conceptual categorization,* in which one experiences *comprehending* through the mind.

Up to about twenty-eight months of age we are pre-perceptual and perceptual, experiencing time in the state of *the watchful present,* a state in which there is no sense that something has happened, a state in which there is a sense of *changeless time.* If we were to regard that changeless time as feeling duration-less, we would call it an *instant of the watchful present.* If we were to regard that changeless time as having duration, we would call it a *period of the watchful present.* Is it helpful to make a distinction between an *instant* of time and a *period* of time? It is to me; as I reckon with the process of revision in which I am inhabiting the space-time of the sentence, I believe the work asks me to *feel*: is this an instant of time and is this a period of time?

Needless to say, pre-perceptual and perceptual categorization fade in us and conceptual categorization often takes precedence. But—and this I believe is important for storytellers to remember: *the pre-perceptual and perceptual states do not disappear.* The child reader remains in the adult reader, more persistently in some adult readers than others, of course.

The mind, a time-traveler

Do you easily travel to the "remembered past" and the "imagined future"? Of course you do—it turns out that, after the organ of the brain is fully developed, its supposed default condition is "future-thinking." It also turns out that the depth of future-thinking is in direct relation to depth of past experience; our sense of what is about to occur is informed by what is past, and this "protention" | "retention" tension is the very essence of "story."

What I'm talking about is what is called "the instinct of futurity." To acknowledge this instinct of futurity in the story's characters is obviously important to inhabiting space-time as they each experience it in different ways.

The instinct of futurity is the plot-and-motive instinct. It's the mind time-traveling to what will be revealed in the future. It's the mind creating future as a *place* from which our experiences will come. We imagine that place, we predict it, we summon it, and then it summons us.

Gaze long and far into the character's instinct of futurity and you begin to feel—very directly and immediately feel—your way further into the sense that the past condition causes the present condition (this is what narratologists call the "causal dilemma").

Gaze long and far into the character's instinct of futurity and you begin to feel your way further into the complex sense that the past condition *and* the imminent condition (the "about-to-be moment") cause the present condition (this is what is called the "causal trilemma").

Gaze long and far at the single sentence conveying space-time—stay there—stay there in order to fully inhabit the ground of the character's ways of being in space-time. Stay there in the space-time of the sentence itself in order to intuitively, consciously, impulsively be *inside* the character's ways of being in space-time.

How long until?

Isn't that the implicit question underlying the first moment of almost every story? Writers live inside that question of temporal duration and temporal estimation as we compose. With luck, each revision takes us deeper inside the question as a drama. And one thing we end up confronting—often in the space-time of a single sentence—is the prospective and retrospective temporal awareness of the character.

Prospective awareness refers to our sense of the *experienced duration*—the sense of a *longer time* passing *now* as attention to many forms of time occurs *within that moment.*

Retrospective awareness refers to our sense of the *remembered duration*—the sense of a longer time having passed *then* (in past experiences) as attention to many forms of time occurred *within that past moment.*

We estimate how long something is lasting or once lasted according to our sense of the *fullness* of the singular moment. The temptation in the final moments of writing a story is to *complete* the singular moment (to allow efficient closure, as if the character—and the reader, too—valued efficiency above all else). If the first and final moments are allowed their *fullness* there will likely be opportunity for the story to convey other dimensions of that "How long until?" question instead of merely answering the question.

The reader's sense of this is often marvelously counterintuitive: the brief sentence that seems to *read slow* will sometimes convey experienced or retrospective duration of great speed; the long sentence that seems to *read fast* will sometimes convey experienced or retrospective duration of great length. Have you had that experience, in which you have known that the pace of a given moment will be sped up if you add more words?

Our sense of *pace* is influenced by matters of *narrative duration*: the relation of our sense of the time it takes to read the narrative to the "story time," the time the story-events themselves lasted. Pace is influenced by *summary duration:* when the reading time is shorter than the "story time"; *ellipses duration*: when the reading time is basically zero, and the story time is longer (as in paragraph breaks, white space breaks, ellipses, some forms of dash, etc.); *scene duration*: when the reading time and the story time are equal; and *stretch duration*: when the reading time is longer than story time.

Once I turned sixty, the matter of the "velocity of living" took on new urgency for me. The matter of "velocity of change" became a more powerful mystery for me than in the recent and distant past. I looked at the clock's hour-measure (that is, the *extensity of time*—my overall sense of its duration) in a different way. I looked at the clock's minute- and second-measures (that is, the *intensity of time*) in a different way. For me, a sentence is, more than ever, a *sentence*, a verdictive experience.

The tempo of a character's life: that's always a part of what we're conveying. A single sentence provides a sense of temporal speed, and, in particular of three influences: *rhythm-oriented experience*: the patterns and the broken patterns inherent in a person's situation; *sequence-oriented experience*: the paths of a person's consciousness as she prioritizes the possibilities before her; and *synchrony-oriented experience:* the ways in which a person's consciousness is attuned to other people's tempos.

Recognizing the prominence of one of these is extraordinarily character-revealing. If, beyond the writer's intention, the story's first sentence asserts that the character is synchrony-oriented, then the characterization of other secondary, tertiary, and supernumerary characters has often already begun in that sentence.

You can shape the sentences to reflect your understanding of the character's relationship to time. "He drank his water and. Now he picked it up." A period after the "and" shapes the language to allow the enigma of the character's identity to shine through.

You write inside the work for the reader. It's up to you as a writer to say, from inside the work, *I believe what the work wants is this.* Are there too many "ands," or is that a special dimension of the work? Do the "ands" occur in all scenes or just one scene? If the "ands" occur only at a scene in the house, you can assume that time and space do not affect the characters when they're in the gym or the forest. Allowing the language to change in those scenes will reveal that something else is going on for the character, that she is experiencing time in a different way, not moment by moment, not in the present.

From *inside* the story, at the sentence-level, reckon with completeness in arcs of development (a moment of becoming) *and* fullness in the spatial-temporal dimension (moments of being).

We waver, we swing

In most circumstances do you concentrate on the present, and are you focused on one activity at a time? In other words, are you *monochronic*? A monochronic person is usually nonlinear since they do not feel the necessity to organize the future and past impinging on the present.

The monochronic person tends to *fill the stillness of time.*

Or, in most circumstances, do you concentrate fairly constantly on the past, the present, and the future, focusing upon several activities at a time? In other words, are you *polychronic*? A polychronic person is usually linear since they *must* learn to be linear in order to survive this condition of the past, present, and future always impinging on one another.

The polychronic person tends to *complete the movements of time.*

Though we may be primarily one or the other—monochronic or polychronic—we shift according to many factors, the most important of which is the particular space we occupy.

You might be monochronic at this moment in a particular chair in that part of the room farthest from the door or the windows. Your jacket, the arms turned inside-out, is on the back of the chair in front of you. You have your bag at your feet. Black faux-leather and pitted with little holes. Now you lift the jacket off the chair and stuff it into your bag. You shift the bag to your lap. You pet it. You say, almost inaudibly, "Yes." A story has begun. The sentences you have written have been, so far, in present tense.

That same story presented in the space-time of a polychronic person would include the past, present, and future always impinging on one another. Your particular chair in that part of the room farthest from the door and far from the windows causes you to remember the front windows of your aunt's home, and for a moment you picture her opening the door of this room. No one was ever a better teacher to you. As you lift the jacket off the chair in front of you and stuff it into your bag, and pet it, you think of her congratulating you, saying, "Yes, *Yes.*" A story has begun.

The sentences you have written have been, so far, in the past tense, which you consistently slide back to from your thoughts of the present and the future and the distant past.

To what degree does our temporal experience reflect our experiences of *natural time (organic time)*; that is, time attuned to the rhythms of nature—the larger seasonal forces, the diurnal and nocturnal behaviors of animal and plant-life?

To what degree does our temporal experience reflect our experiences of time attuned to *mechanical time (inorganic time)*—the routines of our work, the rituals of scheduling, the time pressures that our machines, small and large, seem to construct for us?

In an era of profound separation of humankind from nature, how convincing is a twenty-first century American character whose behavior reflects only natural time? How believable is a twenty-first century American character whose behavior reflects only mechanical time in an era in which nature is powerfully asserting its intimate relationship to—and imminent danger to—humans arrogant enough to think they are insulated from that essential relationship?

Our sentences are tracking and sometimes embodying how time forms, deforms, and reforms according to just two orientations: *ego-moving* and *time-moving*.

The Wednesday Meeting problem is frequently cited in contemporary studies of time orientation. Next Wednesday's meeting has had to be moved forward by two days. What day is the meeting happening now?

If you say "Monday," you are in a *time-moving orientation*. You feel time is moving, that the future is coming toward you. As far as you're concerned, it's all about the future.

If you say "Friday," you are in an *ego-moving* orientation. You feel *you* are actively moving along a timeline toward the future. As far as you're concerned, it's all about *you*.

Of course your specific situation in space is really important to how you answered, as are other factors—of culture and milieu, of power or powerlessness, of gender—that shape the way you inhabit space-time. That *transpersonal temporal sensitivity* is a constant aspect of time orientation.

We are always reckoning with experiences of the dynamic balance between the rhythms of breathing, eating, and sensing, and the rhythms of cultural and social life. How time is experienced in these microtemporal and macrotemporal aspects of life is a natural part of the sense in all living organisms that we are *oscillating*. It is our basic pulse. We waver. We swing. We experience *polysemous time* (the sense that our slightest oscillations keep us swinging from the past to the present to the future, from the future to the present to the past).

In your world-making as you write, do you generously invite reaction—aliveness of thought—and response—somatic aliveness—to depictions and descriptions of space and time, as they function differently in each element of setting?

Trying to patiently reckon with the character's sense of temporal duration, estimation, orientation, and categorization, we are always reckoning with the wide spectrum of stable and unstable temporal logic specific to that unique person in various unique situations. To some degree the sentence we write is a translation of that temporal logic. The sentence has to acknowledge three key aspects of temporal experience: *continuity*—the sense, the elusive (and some would say illusory) sense that there is a *flow* (a definable arc, a shape) in how I experience space-time; *succession*—the sense that we experience time in a succession of stabilizing and destabilizing that both seeks and resists forming a pattern; and *simultaneity*—the sense that the experiences of the past always exist inside the envelope of the future, that the experiences of the future always exist inside the envelope of the present.

All of our self-torturing about the *tense* of our story: it's an acknowledgement that there is so little "tense logic" in temporal logic.

I'm not suggesting we should memorize all this technical vocabulary and make deadly rules for ourselves about the application of it. I'm simply saying that it is never time wasted to slow down and, from within the work, to ask whether the character is—in that particular space-time—feeling that it is all about him, or all about the future.

Experiencing prehensive solitary rapture, the reader feels the full scale of self-love.

Experiencing prehensive communal horror, the reader feels the full scale of love for humanity.

In modern American literature we have often emphasized odd ideas of efficiency that have led us to assume the reader cannot abide biding. We ask writers to *get to it* in the first moments of the poem or story. Yet, many of our poems and stories wish to give witness to the embodying of and the enacting of dawning awareness and, particularly, self-awareness. When we are composing and revising this kind of work, our attention to the coming-to-an-end moment is related to the attention we give the about-to-be-moment. If we hurry past the about-to-be-moment, we create in the reader the expectation of hurrying past the coming-to-an-end moment.

If I could set no other goal for myself fifty years into my just-now-maturing and not-too-late life as a writer, it would be this: *bide* wherever the story or poem has moved past a process of uncovering to a process of discovering; *abide* there.

The force of inverse proportion

Most contemporary American short-short fiction constructs a "flash-flash-and-suddenly-flash-and-suddenly" structure. When I hear people admiringly describe their favorite short-short stories as highly compressed long stories I always want to ask—in a flash and suddenly—"So what earns your highest praise, then, is concentrated substance?"

And as for poems—are brief poems ever praised for being only so much concentrated soap, only the smallest amount needed for your whole head and body?

Likewise, the tendency is to define the novella form purely by length. But is a butterfly simply a compressed version of a bird?

Be attentive to your assumptions about the nature of beauty, especially about the values of beauty.

Both the short-short story and the novella invite the author to acknowledge that the story portraying a shift in *ways of being* is as powerful for many readers as the story portraying a shift in *ways of becoming*. In the short-short story, the author can radically commit to the force of the inverse proportion; that is, to the power of the infinitesimal to reflect the infinite. The novella is an ideal form for commitment to big scale (thematic and psychological depth) in smaller size, an invitation to the reader to *feel* the infinite through abiding presence to the infinitesimal.

The immured condition

Occasionally, I give myself the task of trying to comprehensively read someone I've only ever read in parts. The first time I sat and read all of Willa Cather, the letters, everything, I was almost at the cellular level changed, because she was writing a kind of story that no one else was writing: a story in which the central figure did not change or develop at all. Everyone around that character changed and developed, but her dilemma was that she did not. Katherine Anne Porter reading Cather said that all her central figures have a quality of heroic fixity. They're fixed in place. That's what makes them heroic. The world is changing around them, and they cannot, or will not, change.

Do you believe that some lives are more shaped by nature than by nurture? By divine forces more than by human? Do you believe some lives are shaped by only one or two crucial relationships? Or by a single obsession rather than by many?

The novella should, in my opinion, invite attention to the character acted upon rather than acting; at the threshold, but not arriving; facing the invitation to transcend or to be destroyed. This invitation may reside in a drama of the body—the singular struggle to be fully alive, the singular struggle to die and be done. Or in a moment of stultification—the stopped or stilled character. Or in the arrival of an Other, a double, a ghost, through which the character will only ever know or meet himself, as with Marlow and Kurtz—the horror; or Scrooge and Tiny Tim—the boy he *was.*

The novella can inspire attention to and even love for the character who might be seen as superficial, an outcast, extraneous to their culture.

Such characters experience the strange gravitations of feeling "immured" (a condition appearing prominently in Joyce's and Katherine Anne Porter's and Marguerite Duras's work and Nin's collection, *Under a Glass Bell*), unable to unbury themselves in their individual lives and in their relationships. The characters' labyrinthine journeys include sensations occurring with such frequency that, as in Virginia Woolf, they are not easily tracked.

The novella form values temporal dilation and compression, often taking place in a very limited span of time, as well as spatial dilation and compression, through close attention to the rhythms and richnesses—the small routines and rituals—of a single setting. A single *confining* setting: the abyss, the place of oblivion—verging on being liberating, but not. Verging on being unsurvivable, but not.

The novella acknowledges enigma of motive as often as it

reveals motive. It shows no outcome as often as it reveals outcome. Stephen Crane called his plots "maps of accidents."

The novella's one character may have had one or two relationships in that lifetime, and now finds all relationships dissolved or dissolving. The tone of examination is often merciless.

The point of view may be self-limiting: the outsider as in Cather, the confused insider as in Melville, the recorder as in Dostoevsky, or the amused omniscient narrator as in O'Connor. This is a narrator not willing to articulate what we know but wishing to admit what we do not. A withholding narrator, who leaves things out. In revising if not in composing, the author strips away the articulating and honors the admitting—evident in white space, in unbuilt transitions, in chapter openings and closings. The author removes emphasis, trusting the reader's direct shared experience.

The novella may offer disproportion of elements; for instance, setting or thought and observation overwhelming the work, the inner story becoming *the* story. Extremes of exposition or evocation, of objectivity or subjectivity, of voice, tone, gaps, and irresolution will test the tolerances of the reader.

The opening of a novella can constitute a dare: will the reader tolerate time with this character? The novellas I most admire challenge us to ask whether our sustained engagement as humans can be given to a person held in a trap.

Elusiveness, inerrancy, oblivion, rapture

In the short-short fiction that most powerfully, pleasurably claims me the *entire story* resides in the about-to-be-moment or in the coming-to-an-end moment. These moments make no effort to speedwalk across great distances and rapidly experience many things; these moments offer time for a single thing with depth and span, including a charged object, to claim you, as Rilke wrote: "In order for a thing to speak to you, you must regard it for a certain time as the only one that exists."

The short-short story often radically commits attention to elements that conventionally are assigned a facilitative role. It is a drama complete unto itself when the talismanic object (something passed from one person to another among family, or the focus of obsession as in Gogol's "Overcoat," and *not* necessarily a symbol) receives the individual's or the group's fixed and sustained attention. In the long story, and novella and novel, object obsession is a compelling drama complementary to larger dramas; the object obsession helps make the work's mysteries recognizable and meaningful. When the short-short story writer fully commits to the singular drama of object obsession by eschewing the presence of other dramas, the work's mysteries can become dreamlike and even mystical. This short-short story moves beyond portraying normal attentiveness to the object; equally it resists portraying abnormal obsession. It honors *normal obsession.*

As this kind of obsession story unfolds, it offers a picture of a marvelously and murderously attentive heart and mind. Without attaching the mechanics of overt background or foreground plot, the story offers the reader a portrait of oblivion (such an abyss, of course, naturally envelopes light) or rapture (such light naturally envelopes the abyss).

An example: A gardener obsesses over a new bulb that arrives. The gardener examines the living bulb, its flesh, its roots, its texture, color, smell. He worries that it mustn't stay in its plastic bag too long, that it must be put in the right cool and dark place until he can plant it. He pictures many possible sites to store it. With extraordinary sadness, he pictures the cold darkness; with extraordinary happiness, he imagines the places he might ultimately plant the bulb. He experiences opposing emotions as he imagines exactly the right place. He then begins imagining the good and terrible possibilities for the actual planting of the bulb, how he must prepare the soil, what he will do about the vole problem.

If such a piece merely establishes a symbolic correspondence (bulb = Lost Mother) it is far less satisfying than if it reminds the reader of the transformative power of an object that is mystical (pushing into but not arriving at meaning; actively resisting meaning). A person not wishing to change will be met by a force of nature (a bulb) ready to transcend dormancy.

The short-short story may also place radical trust in both the enchanted setting and the enchanted moment. Nothing at all dramatic happens in this one place at this one moment though it is understood that the ensorcelling place and time shift the person's ways of being.

These reading experiences have in them the echoes of fairy tales since they cast a spell over the reader; like certain kinds of fairy tales and fables, they will sometimes include a final comment (and/or a "moral to the story," as in, "Sometimes you will find a girl like a grasshopper whom you think is a bell cricket") that briefly, incidentally acknowledges plot. They draw some of their incantatory power from an enchanted setting and a magic time. The central figure in such stories feels like a participant *and* a nonparticipant, which is characteristic of most dream experiences.

Knowledge and enlightenment (as in recognizable story *theme*) are *not* the natural desired outcome for the reader of this particular story form; rather, this story form offers "sabi," as in its classical definition from 1689: the state of spiritual serenity resulting from the pleasurable and/or disturbing encounter with "the egoless, impersonal life of nature"—an intimate, lasting experience of dreamlike disturbance and surprise and, at last, uncanny serenity.

The short-short story form can invite the author to trust the presentation of documents and statements and declarations as reflections of severely limited human engagement. The writer recognizes that a document or statement or declaration conceding no possibility of error and providing no opportunity for response has created a compelling, provocative closed system.

For example: a set of instructions for use of the restroom hand dryer; these instructions will leave no doubt about the *one* way to activate the dryer, the *one* way to dry each hand, the *one* dangerous thing you must not do when using the hand dryer, the *one* result of overuse of the dryer, etc. The document has the essence of *story* according to the degree that it suggests the tension of struggles against absolute authority. In the hair dryer instructions that state what *must happen* resides the plot of what *has happened* in that tribe; the cold ashes of the inerrant hair dryer instructions suggest the fire endured by a person or persons who disregarded the instructions.

Communication that occurs in a naturally brief form (journal entries, postcards, emails, online postings, professional and personal memos, or letters of application) often has a context that is elusive for both the receiver and the sender, for the writer and for the intended audience. For example: a person sending three postcards from the Louvre tells about seeing the three paintings on the postcards, and is including personal information that implies a process of growing self-understanding and/or growing self-delusion; the audience for the postcards might be implicitly involved in resolving conflict with the postcard writer or might be involved in escalating conflict with the postcard writer; the postcard writer might seem to be writing to themself as well as to the addressee.

The epistolary form reminds readers of how we find drama

"beneath the lines." The intensity of implication increases when we have only a partial document: only three of five postcards (two that have been referred to but were never received); three postcards but not the responding postcards; three postcards that are sent to three different people with very different iterations of the same message; three postcards that are sent just before or just after the climactic events that would occur in the context of a much, much larger set of dramas than those referred to (directly or indirectly) in the postcards.

Effective transaction of "story" is not the pleasure of this short-short form. Ineffective and broken transaction of story are the appeal for the reader. The power of elusiveness is the reward in the beginning, middle, and end of this form.

Reading experiences of this kind call to mind traditions of storytelling in which the original document has eroded (as in sacred texts discovered in an advanced state of decay) but faith has been placed in wild surmise; or in which memory of the whole story has not been preserved (as in the oral traditions of disappearing tribes and dissolving communities and families, as in the recollections of someone with a form of brain syndrome) but there is reverence expressed in the partial account; or in which the trickster or fool deliberately hides the whole story from view, offering only one rich morsel of the whole feast; or in which a witness gives testimony that is sparse and fragmentary and puzzling but upon which others will depend for an important overall assumption of "guilt" or "innocence."

I believe good short-short stories arise from full presence to the substructural mysteries; great short-short stories arise from *radical* presence to those substructural mysteries. The masterpieces of short-short fiction arise from radical presence to the *rhythms* of these substructural mysteries.

Breaching the bolted door

Beneath the face you show to everyone and to yourself is a different face, and beneath that face is another. You are able to acknowledge your own cognitive dissonances in a general way that helps you honorably imply to everyone and to yourself: *This is my true nature.* If you are a caregiver attuned to the dignity of those you serve, you show your respect: *This is my professional demeanor.* As time passes, you live with growing suspicion that you are never quite telling the truth because you actively postpone facing the profound contradictions evident in your hidden-most face.

The more actively you hide this face over time, the more likely it will inevitably come to meet you. If what seems most recognizable about you is your calmness and fearlessness, what will come to meet you in your life will be a figure of disturbance and terror. If what seems most recognizable about you is your disturbing and terrifying nature, what will come to meet you in your life will be a figure of calmness and fearlessness. This is what the ancient Greeks called *enantiodromia.*

Your relationship of mutually assured destruction with your in-law is a relationship confounding and perfectly understandable because each of you can(not) believe that your Other/Familiar has come to meet you: your *double.* A Gerasim will come to meet an Ivan Ilyich. A Kurtz will come to meet a Marlow. A Billy Budd will come to meet a Captain Veer. A woman locked up for The Cure will find another woman—unrecognizable and impossibly recognizable—in the yellow wallpaper of her place of confinement. A Beloved comes to meet Sethe. A Giovanni will come to meet

David. The warrior who has confirmed what everyone thought about him—and, indeed, what he thought about himself—as he defeated the beast Grendel, must confront *the mother* of Grendel, which means that what was hidden behind Grendel was what waited to meet the warrior.

As I wrote the novel *One Kind Favor*, which is a sustained ghost story set in contemporary North Carolina, I put myself through my paces in trying to generatively reflect on what forces bring ghosts from behind bolted doors. Ghosts are not artifacts of old superstitions. Called by specific internal and external phenomena, they ride our breaths, and we see them appear and disappear as if we were outside in freezing temperatures, as if they were coming from us, as if they were coming back into us.

At the beginning of *One Kind Favor*, the murder of Lincoln Lennox is introduced as a dramatic element. Lincoln is a character who links the other characters together—but after the first pages, he is absent from the primary and secondary dramas; he is only a presence in the real focus of the work, which is the carnival of wonder and horror taking place in an American town where the hate impulse has revived the ghosts of the murdered and of the dead murderers, and now makes ghosts of the so-called living. As in work by Washington Irving and Mark Twain and Toni Morrison and William Faulkner, the *uncanny* marks the spell the town is under: nothing makes sense.

Until I can understand from inside the characters' experiences that the place they live is paradoxical, I don't feel like the work is authentic, even believable. The most important settings for *One Kind Favor* are Ephesus Swamp and the consignment-bar Stanley'sAcker'sStanley's and the Helltel. They are haunted places, and the reader residing in them feels sensitized to sounds that are summoned and that arise unbidden. I hope that the reader feels how time is deformed in these places: the swamp, a place of decay and death—and redemption; the consignment-bar, a place with no redemptive future—a place in which a line has been drawn through the past and future and what remains is the ruined present; the Helltel, the crypt welcoming dead and living wayfaring strangers. I hope that the reader, held captive in these places, more or less constantly wonders (and worries), "Did I hear what I thought I heard?"

One Kind Favor is an Alice in Wonderland experience in which the adult reader is asked to recover fully the child reader inside: the reader who wishes her body to come alive inside the body of language; the reader who welcomes the invitation of storytelling to produce altered states that turn you and your world inside-out, that invite you to wisdom through nonsense and silliness.

The wit, the butt, and the laugher

Working within the challenges of the comic mode has allowed me to push myself further into my obsession with understanding the nature of fiction that is *felt* first and *thought* next by the reader, that is the cause of prehension—the "something there" sensation—as well as comprehension.

Our laughter is, for the most part, a physical response over which we have little and sometimes, no control.

Here is a fairly weak joke:

A man driving around and around, looking for a parking space, says, "God, what I wouldn't give—I'd change my ways—I'd go to more lectures—I'd become a Christian for just one parking space. Just one!" Instantly, a parking space appears! The driver pulls in, says, "Found one! Never mind!"

Kafka would ask, "Is that supposed to be funny?" In Kafka

and Isaac Babel and Gogol the story would end with the character saying, "A space, at last!" and, indignantly, "Did you see that? Are you paying attention at all, God?" just as the car locks clicked down, and the heater came on.

Anaïs Nin would ask, "Is that story fully embodied?" In Nin and Angela Carter (and, perhaps, Stuart Dischell and Tom Lux) the driver would be a naked woman, experiencing naugahyde orgasm, and she would be praying to the stink-eyed dog giving birth *and* dying on the curb.

In Flann O'Brien and Samuel Beckett and Stanley Elkin *God* would be hoping for the parking space. When vast numbers of spaces instantly appeared, God would take the one space in which a human had parked. God would banish the human from it forever, and perform a miracle on the dog.

If we find one version funnier than another we must ask why. Baudelaire would remind us that "neither laughter nor tears are to be seen in the paradise of all delights. They are both of them the children of suffering, and occur only when the human body is unable to restrain them." In our ways of valuing literary works of various kinds, we seem to trust tears more than we do laughter.

I find Baudelaire's distinctions helpful. I'm summarizing him: In joy we feel a unity of inward responses. In laughter we feel what he calls "the revelation of a double, not to say a self-contradictory, sentiment." Joy usually manifests itself in the grin or smile that is involuntary, a response that is not as "convulsive" and childlike as laughter.

In most instances, laughter alone and laughter in public make children of the laughers. Laughter is the body's judgment of experiences in ways that compromise the adult's will to *withhold* judgment. (You didn't judge the man, the woman, the God in the car? I think you did.) I hold with Baudelaire, Kerr, Bergson, and a raft of philosophers that we are adults *judging* in almost godlike ways when we read; when we laugh as we read, we judge in almost doglike ways. Baudelaire wrote, "The Being who wished to multiply His creatures in his own image, did not give to men the teeth of the lion—but laughter is men's way of biting." The butt of the joke, the wit shaping the joke, the laughers present for the joke, have all directly or indirectly created a context for *biting*, which is to say a social context that is either overtly or covertly corrective, that configures a moral stance, that echoes the drama of tragedy.

Kafka, Babel, Gogol, Nin, Carter, O'Brien, Beckett, Elkin, and so many others would assert: the comic always derives from the tragic.

Charlie Chaplin understood that; depending on your preferences, you might say Buster Keaton understood it even better than Chaplin. But. But, I'm God-damned if I don't mention that the issue of God significantly complicates our sense of the tragic. It does, of course. Many writers and philosophers have insisted, in fact, that tragedy, understood classically, simply does not exist for the masses in organized religion because organized religion has made them believe that all manifestations of destructiveness and self-destructiveness can be considered insignificant, at last, from the modern God's perspective. From the modern God's perspective, they would say, everything appearing tragic is only, after all, a slight injury humans exaggerate, treat as grave: bathos.

From compassion for those who proudly consider their modern Gods as merciless as the gods of the ancients, let's agree to this broad distinction in the forms of tragedy and comedy: in comedy the hero—in soul if not body, in body if not soul—survives the most profound woundings; and those around the comic hero survive. In tragedy the hero and some if not all of the hero's loved ones are destroyed body and soul.

No escape clause

How does the writer give the comic its full value?

From the very beginning of the work there can be no flinching in committing to humor's malicious intent. It is okay to bark, to nip, to gnaw, but do not hold back *biting*. Do not underestimate the need for readers to acknowledge what Walter Kerr calls the "holy improprieties" of comedy:

1) Comic Exposure. Invite us to laugh at outward deformity—what? you don't laugh at Cyrano's nose? at the hair, hands, and mouths of O'Connor's and Welty's characters? Invite us to enact this comic exposure and you create recognition in us of our companionship in despair. O'Connor, so taken with Christian ritual enactment of suffering, unflinchingly invites this unholy communion. Welty, her sensibility so shaped by early life in the community of Jackson, Mississippi, by her experiences as a journalist and as a publicity agent and photographer for the WPA, unflinchingly invites this sense of unseemly citizenship. In their best work both make us feel wicked, righteous, corrupt, holy, sacrilegious.

2) Compound Despair. Look for opportunities the situation creates for the character's despair to be multiplied, as Flann O'Brien clearly has done in *The Third Policeman*. Nathanael West seems a direct descendent of Gogol in his skill at multiplying the quotidian indignities and humiliations. Isaac Babel and Ambrose Bierce show us how the waiting for death and the bargaining and negotiating with God or the devil is far worse for some soldiers than death itself or any final judgment could possibly be. We're thankful, aren't we, when someone like Stanley Elkin, as if carrying Mark Twain's comic DNA, reminds us that a comic hero's suicide attempts are just funny, tragically, terribly funny. The poison tastes really awful, and the comic hero just can't drink it all. He should have bought

Saran Wrap instead of a Ziploc bag. The gas he turned on is—*quite unexpectedly*—making him too sick to finish his suicide poem. He has rope but his knot-making ability was never good, and the friend he has brought to help is, well, suicidal.

3) Beware the Emotional Escape Clause. Groucho Marx made a distinction between an amateur and a professional working in the comic mode. Here is how Walter Kerr tells the story: "An amateur thinks it's funny, Groucho said, if you dress a man up as an old lady, put him in a wheel chair, and give the wheel chair a push that sends it spinning down a slope toward a stone wall. For a pro, Groucho said, it's got to be a *real* old lady." Those of us trying to give comedy its full power cannot insulate the effect. Think about how brutal W.C. Fields (with that smug, self-involved face exactly like Dick Cheney's face) could be, though no less brutal than any of us can also be. Asked if there should be clubs for young people, Fields said, "Only when kindness fails." Thinking on it a single beat longer our laughter disappears. We tell the story to someone else; our laughter, which we might wish to suppress, reappears. A work like Twain's *The Man Who Corrupted Hadleyburg* is simply merciless. It is a long story no doubt because Twain wanted the larger scale in order to have full opportunity to leave unturned no single stone covering the hypocrisy's ugly stains. Injured dignity has comic power because dignity itself is such a pressing fundamental human need. Injure some dignity—with no escape clause.

4) Remember the Ampersand. The Four and then the Three Marx Brothers, The Three Stooges, Monty Python, the Not-Ready-for-Primetime Players, Bob & Ray, Nichols & May. Another way of compounding despair without falling into the trap of the emotional escape clause is to multiply characters, to crowd the work, introducing more minor characters than you normally might, more groups of minor characters, giving ludicrously generous attention to minor

character relationships that will surprise us by defying the expectation that they remain in the background. Allow both late-arriving and early-departing major and minor characters. Grace Paley says she lets two stories collide, but I suspect she then starts to look for the third force. In a dynamic of three characters, she will put together that classic combination of wit, butt, and laugher (the echo of author/character/reader, of course), or she will put together wit, wit, and lesser wit (often a male), or she will put together butt, butt, and butt (often they will all be members of the same family).

5) Acknowledge the Magic, Hostile, Disharmonious Environment around the Comic Hero. Give attention to its strange features and operations. Your dorm bed and pillow covered in surprisingly slippery plastic, the wasp that stings you when your softball team really, really needs your support: all of us can relate to how *painfully* humorous it is to have to acknowledge that Olympus is different than we might have anticipated.

Acknowledge the mechanical qualities of the world that make clowns of us: the watch, the palm pilot, the cell phone, the television, all of which are smarter than the user. Use a cane short enough and you begin to look as much like a camera tripod as a human. Wear a very stiff tie, you look like a clock stuck on the hour of twelve. Laughter is often caused by us seeing a person as what Henri Bergson calls "a jointed puppet," a "human body made laughable in exact proportion as that body reminds us of a mere machine."

In the eternity of *The Third Policeman* it is simply assumed that all people are what the narration calls "constituent" people: some percentage of each of them is bicycle. Some bicycles have what is called a "high content of humanity."

If this causes us delight it might just be because we recognize that our lives in our bodies are so often like bad dreams. The drag on our bodies and from our various physical costumes and disguises and from our most common gestures is part of a losing battle with nature, a debacle we *would* be constantly aware of if we did not live so absent-mindedly. Our laughter shakes us out of the insensibility we live in for so many hours; it invites us to be more fully alive, less mechanical, less automatic.

Let the body laugh at the mind

Language, of course, verges into and out of having or lacking "a high content of humanity."

Consider how flawed intellectual connections in language and false artificiality of expression and false rationalizing language are fairly constant in how we humans treat language. We have almost daily practice hearing something we ourselves or someone else has said that "strikes" us as funny, and we involuntarily laugh. In order to invite laughter from the reader, we might—where the work will accommodate this—wish to consider making the very paths of the sentences more broken in syntax; we might wish to give the artificial expressions of jargon and default expression more attention; in revision we might expand the passages of thought that involve body and mind in riddling conflict with each other.

I know my own body responds strangely to this marvelous real three-word offer: *microsurgical vasectomy reversals.* My laughter really does come from my uneasy body. Only then does my mind start to consider it: Very small tools used on very small tools.

My body responds to this fictional offer: *macrocolonoscopic dilation.* It is not the language I respond to with my upper body. Really. Thus: low comedy.

In the spirit of play that is part of the joy of writing in the comic mode, let's alter that first one only slightly to *discount* microsurgical vasectomy reversals. Let's alter that second one to *epic* macrocolonoscopic *marination*. Is our laughter different? Does the terminology almost simultaneously offer experiences of high and low comedy?

Where you have had these procedures—a Tijuana pharmacy—a fiction workshop—matters more to the humor, right? In the language there is both more to feel and more to think. The *felt* and the *thought* are in vergence, in what Henri Bergson would call "reciprocal interference," the dynamic state in which "one of two comedies is on the point of upsetting the other." And if the comic writer is not willing to welcome those kinds of interferences, to allow line-level *instabilities* to push those limits, the work is less likely to surprise either in dialogue or narration or scene.

When the material before you is in the comic mode, do you find that all your jig inventions are high-comic jigs employed to realize the cerebral, aesthetic, ironic qualities of that material's substance and form? Does that same material have the potential for low comedy? And do you invent low-comedy jigs in order to fully realize the visceral, erotic, paradoxical qualities of your work?

Going, again, to the example of our own lives for the richness we reach for in our stories and poems, consider the patterns that no sooner form than they break. Our own incorrigibility awareness and our own corrigibility awareness—our awareness of what cannot be set right and what can be set right—is comic when most intensely tragic, tragic when most intensely comic.

In exposing ripening inevitabilities, in showing the compounding absurdities of failing connection, in depicting the sense of entrapment that the characters themselves have created, storytelling can cause in the reader the convulsion of laughter or the silent burp of a smile or the flinching inner smile, the tearing that occurs when we feel in the same moment the gravity and the risibility of it all, the tearing that occurs as we laugh and as we regret laughing. When a writer has before them the imminent or desinent moment, it is worth considering this form of reversal: at the about-to-be moment or the coming-to-an-end moment in a tragic story, welcome in the comic mode; welcome in the tragic mode at the about-to-be moment or the coming-to-an-end moment in a comic story.

I have wished to comment on the nature of laughter as a response to literature: the body's unique wisdom expressed; the reader's Godlike judgment of our human self-contradictions; the reader's doglike, biting corrective response generated by the situation of a wit, a butt, a laugher enacting our *almost* unsurvivable tragic situations; the reader's convulsive body reminding them not to value tears over laughter, not to assume the tragic does not inhabit the comic.

We *bite* and *bite* and *bite* at the vivid pictures of our human impersonality, our superiority, our machine nature, the qualities that remind us of our distance from what we might *feel.* Our biting laughter does not feel individual. It has a way of making us feel part of a scary, beautiful, howling pack. We ask the laughing readers to feel complicit *in their very flesh and bones* with all the other laughers experiencing so much deeply felt grace and joy that we know cannot last—and so much deeply felt degradation and horror that is enduringly unbearable.

In waves, the artist's love
uncovers the greater loves.

In waves, the greater loves
uncover the artist's loves.

The fatal gaze

The interviewer asked, "Have you ever fallen in love?"

What a marvelous question for a storyteller who has, unexpectedly, lived to be nearly seventy. The echoes of that question ring in all the chambers behind me, the chambers ahead, the chamber I now inhabit. As sincerely as I am able, I will speak from within the echoes.

I have learned that in order to "fall" in love, I must be ready to no longer live in the perfect balance of self-absorption in which falling does not include the outcomes of actual failing. I must choose to "fail" in clinging to my own definitions for and my own conditions of love. The very reason I committed my life—over fifty years ago—to storytelling is because of my belief in the path of reckoning inherent in the question, *Have you ever fallen-failed-fallen in love?*

I believe this particular question is the essential question of storytelling across every culture in every era. The motives of protagonists and antagonists are reflected in the urgency of that question; the outcomes of their falling-failing-falling actions are linked to the mysteries of the question; the reader's sense of the comic and tragic implications of the story is informed by the reader's awareness of the question's significance in the story's milieu. I dare you to try to subtract that question from any work of literature that has claimed you and that echoes in you. The question is always present in us.

In our own twenty-first century of extremely polarized camps, shouldn't each of us value more than ever this life-transforming question? In our personal and public relationships, we have the opportunity to move beyond the life-stunting questions: Are you The Other I fear? Are you The Enemy I should wall out? Why should your life matter as much as mine? Why won't you respect my beliefs?Have you ever fallen-failed-fallen in love? is good ground upon which to experience "the fatal gaze"; that is, the intense concentration that will murder your false assumptions about yourself and others. Whether you have asked or have only thought the question, you must confront your own readiness to gaze further inside than ever before. When you gaze past the life-stunting battery of questions, you begin to recover the one life-giving question.

When you have recovered the question that matters most, your impulse to look beyond yourself is, at first, an agitating and disturbing falling-out-of-your-own-perceived-condition.

Your self-forgetting then brings a painful and equally pleasurable experience of shedding expectations and assumptions.

As that new impulse intensifies, you look and look and look again at the person before you; you feel how that new impulse to be fully present will undermine your habits of looking swiftly past the person before you. When your looking-looking-looking becomes gazing-looking-gazing, you feel a melting-away of the identity you constructed for that person. You begin to cross out of yourself, to *fall* out of yourself into a loving self that does not at all—and will not ever—feel "safe" but that feels just and right.

If you retreat from the fatal gaze, you will try again. If you will stay on the ground of the question, you will retreat but you will try again—with greater courage and conviction—to experience your loving self. Finally, you will find that loving self makes it possible for you to fearlessly *enter* the condition of the person before you, to *inhabit* that person's ways of falling-failing-falling in love.

In the next moment, you *become* the person before you. The

context now exists for you to value that person as never before, to find new definitions of and conditions for loving that person.

Have you experienced this in literature, when you are sure you have entered and, in fact, have *become* the central character? Sula (in Toni Morrison's *Sula*), Esperanza (in Sandra Cisneros's *The House on Mango Street*), Anna (in Tolstoy's *Anna Karenina*), Rio and Pucha (in Jessica Hagedorn's *Dogeaters*), Thomas and Beulah (in Rita Dove's *Thomas and Beulah*). Storytelling has, then, given you—as it has given me—a method of loving. Do I believe that this "method" is life-altering?

Yes. Yes! Yes.

How grateful I am for the question, which has echoed through every page of my life!

Trespass vision, and the yearning to know

One of the breakthrough stages of growth for me as a writer occurred when I wrote *Little Peg.* The protagonist of that novel has experienced PTSD as a result of her brother and her husband being emotionally scarred soldiers who have returned from the Vietnam War. Peg is a person capable of fierce and articulate rage and tender and inarticulate love. If not for the wives, mothers, sisters, and daughters of Vietnam vets who allowed me to extensively interview them and, in some cases, re-interview them, my novel's portrayal of Peg would have been softer by far—and more false: a patriarchal construction of her life in which I brought to bear my own unearned and dishonest sense of her condition instead of Peg's own earned sense of in-your-face honesty and openness. When I would bring chapter drafts to these women readers, they would firmly remind me that portraying Peg as likeable would not in any way make her authentic. They fundamentally changed my way of valuing (instead of understating) the character's otherness. They changed me forever as an artist who wishes to hold himself responsible for the work while also utterly disappearing behind it.

As a novelist I do not seek out the stories that I can master but the stories that will master me. In my novel *One Kind Favor*, the story would neither allow me to look away from its darkness nor to excuse my agency in that darkness.

I'm pretty sure that I'm like many other writers in having dialogue with my characters during the hours—of the day and the hours of the night and quite often during the dream hours—that I'm not making sentences. That ongoing dialogue makes me aware of the boundaries around all characters in my fiction, and the invitation to exercise "trespass vision" (Tillie Olsen's term) *only* with conscious awareness of limits. I'm lucky as a writer to live in this historical moment when courageous activists, who are in intimate dialogue with erased members of our community, chant "Say her name."

I was in years of dialogue with the young Black character Lincoln Lennox who has been lynched, learning from that daily connection that I cannot ever know him except as an embodied absence. That's a limit—acknowledged in every page of my novel—that causes me to ache. The writing has come from the aching and yearning to feel more deeply and to know more vulnerably; the writing has not come from the need to generalize and to claim authority.

Looking for MOM

When I'm researching, I am in the practice of honoring particularities. Rather than research a place, an era, a person, or an incident for the sake of feeling generally grounded, I am trying to stay alert to the *ungrounding* detail. In other words, I'm trying to earn the right to make the fictional world, but I am limiting my research to the particulars that inform the mysteries of that fictional world.

Writing *One Kind Favor*, I had in mind a specific North Carolina small town. I visited it in person so I could take in with all my senses the ungrounding details. I visited it through at least eleven full rounds of reading research, so I could feel informed about mysteries, and particularly informed by the mysteries that seemed unanswerable.

I *found* the fictional town Cord. I did not find it through orienting or establishing notes but through notes generating processes of questioning. *Does it matter,* I wrote, *that the pines surrounding the swamp at the edge of town are slash pines?* I wrote, *Why barbed wire at all the outer boundaries of the swamp—keeping-in wire or keeping-out?—or once for keeping-in and now for keeping-out?* I asked, *The town's yearly festival—a ceremony enacting what paradoxes.*

What are the strange mysteries in the *milieu* as reflected by the ceremony of the town festival? What are the *outcomes* of a town's economy being tied to pine needles? What are the *motives* for the barbed wire?

You could say I was constructing Cord as the story was creating it.

I take it as a given that in all my processes of pre-composing, composing, and revising I will try to be alert to strangeness that brings aliveness to my storytelling by creating both receptivity and resistance in that story's terms of engagement. In all phases of writing and research I give high priority to the discovery of the transformative strangeness evident in three specific areas I consider elemental to the proportions of a story: motive, outcome, milieu. As a playful, helpful mnemonic I remind myself that I'm "looking for MOM."

I've learned to acknowledge that there are rich paradoxes in how the various elements are counterintuitively linked: milieu to motive, milieu to outcome, outcome to motive.

Look for motive—and questions pertaining to it—at the sentence level. Observe the outcome of the smallest present-action things the character does, including the altering of others' perceptions. (Action and speech are outcomes but so are two others that are more hidden—non-action and gesture; gesture is more expressive than speech, and it's more revealing than actions.) Pay attention to the penetration of the milieu into the moment—the outside world present, not as trigger, but simply there, in the character's consciousness.

In choosing the sentences to examine, look for those with a strong sense of fullness as opposed to completeness. Creating fullness has to be trusted sentence by sentence, and then adjusted toward better fullness. Deep examination of a small single thing—one sentence—creates explosive impulsion—tight coiling—for the piece that will arise from it.

The writer's job is to pay attention to the moments.

The writer's courage is tested at the level of the sentence.

Seek the interbeing

Enter and inhabit what is before you. Encounter the "interbeing"—the Zen Buddhist teacher Thich Nhat Hahn's term for awareness of all beings and awareness of self *at the same time*—that exists between the writer and the character. (Thich Nhat Hahn explained that he coined the term as an attempt to describe the deep connection—at the cellular level—between the world around us and what we perceive of as our separate self. He said, "There are no solitary beings. The whole planet is one giant, living, breathing cell, with all its working parts linked in symbiosis.")

Consciously seek and enter the interbeing before writing. To find the interbeing, listen for a "root note," a tuning fork, *in the sentence* rather than in the whole book or the point of view or other concepts. When you can say, "This sentence feels like the one," rewrite it, recopy it.

Writing "style" might be only another way of describing the evidence on the page of how a writer moves through their own sensibility, their own ways of being and becoming, of holding themself at a certain distance from their own interior worlds and the realms of experience around them. For most of us that sensibility is joined to, though not exclusively consistent with, our artistic sensibility, our sense of beauty, our capacity for standing in the middle distance between our lived experience and the story we will make of it. What the writer wishes to find in the material is a *third* sensibility: the interbeing. A "writing style" might then be said to be the fingerprint of these interpenetrating sensibilities. We know as we read each other's work that we are in varying degrees encountering the person, the artist, and the interbeing that has the DNA of both but has become neither.

Allow exploration of that which is *created* by the interbeing as opposed to *constructed* by the willful author. The impulse to control, to complete, shuts out the interbeing.

Looking for DAD

Your questions of narrative technique will be answered by narrative sensibility.

Revision by the sentence—vertical revision—sensitizes the ear to the rhythm of the word clusters. In this way, the writer can regain childlike wonder and recharge authorial generosity.

From courage and generosity come variations in narrative distance leading to dynamic balance. I think of these as making up a second mnemonic I rely on—DAD: distance, authorial generosity, and dynamic balance. Narrative distance of course refers to things seen objectively or subjectively, but might also be thought of as the aesthetic versus the erotic condition—aesthetic, the sense that things can be seen completely; erotic, the sense of fullness but not completeness.

Dynamic balance is the experience of the uncertain—charged—moment, a sensation partly a matter of the pleasure of its singing. I don't mean "balance" as in symmetry or proportionality. I mean *dynamic* balance, as in falling-into-balance and falling-out-of-balance at the same moment.

Believe that readers are inherently generous; this makes authorial generosity more possible.

Sensory detail, attended to with authorial generosity, stops the narrative to destabilize it, for a moment. Test your sentences for the "delicate object," the cause or trigger for profound ingression or progression. Are there enough, and where do they occur? Do these levers allow instability—chaos—even for a few words?

A natural richness in our lives is in moments of chaos within stability. These occur best at small rather than large, dramatic moments. Very momentary instability energizes the reader—by creating somatic engagement—even without attracting their attention.

Allow the interbeing to go where the work will go, including unlikely focal points, expansive moments that seem pointless, and intermodal shifts (the comic within tragic, for example). The writer, generous, is potentially drawn—through presence—deeper into the darkness or deeper into the light.

The tension between the two extremes is in the writer.

The will of the work, the will of writer

I believe a manuscript represents a dynamic convergence of the author's will, the will of the work itself, and the will of the reader.

The reader wishes for fiction to generate comprehensible and ineffable human mysteries; to welcome the inward and outward journeys that are resolvable (comic) and irreconcilable (tragic); and to sound language's clear root notes, its chords, and its engaging, estranging silences.

The work itself wishes to present the spectacles of becoming and the dramas of being; to reveal the selves, the illusions of self, and the true self of the characters and the world of the characters; to be a living organism that invites physical responses (prehensions), as well as cerebral reactions (comprehensions); and to assume flexible structures and patterns that reflect literature as an invitation to lose and to recover innocence.

The author wishes to relent to the generous will of the work and to the generous will of the reader for whom the work itself exists.

The editor has no other wish than to be at the service of the willing work, the willing artist, and, by implication, the willing reader.

A draft represents a process of discovery, about the characters—voice, perspective, ways of being—but equally about you as a writer and as a person. What do you seem to intuitively *value* in this particular work, and how is your *will* asserting itself? In looking at your completed draft, notice, *first,* what you control and fail to control; your relationship to the characters, the story, and its audience; your stance, your distance, your philosophy (or the absence of any of these) and your role in the world of this work—are you transcriber? Translator? Transformer?

In strategizing your revision beyond the sentence level, locate where the language lifted off (or failed to), and where the perspective intensified (or de-intensified). Recognize the value of minor characters, and ask yourself if there's a need for more crowding. Recognize the value of gross and specific settings, noticing what is vague and asking yourself why. Recognize movement through time and space, asking yourself if space-time is overfocused or under-focused, and notice opportunities for conflation, compression, and expansion.

Then you are prepared for cutting away large passages; adding significant new material such that proportions are shifted; crowding, reversing, reordering, recasting—and in that process, discovering the shape of the story or colliding stories.

Everyone says universally to writers, "How do you know when you're done?" And writers who are honest always say, "I never know when I'm done. I just have a sense that I've brought to bear all of the skills I have at that moment and am honest with myself about that."

The dynamic balance of the disadvantageous

All well-made and well-crafted kites, gates, fences, arches, bridges, and spider webs are occasional structures. All twenty-first century art is made on the occasion of The Singularity—the moment in history when there is as much artificial intelligence present in the world as human intelligence.

Has there ever been an occasion in which artists and artisans are more at risk of oblivion? Does this thought cause you pleasure? To be at that brink: it's a genuinely liberating thought, isn't it?

At all points in our lives as artisans as we reckon with the occasional structures, we are reckoning with our assumptions about *utilitarian form*; that is, form following function. We tend to learn first how to make the transfunctional thing, the thing that combines functions for multiple advantages. Our cellphones are multifunctional media centers; our trifocals address three focalizing challenges. We often tend to respond to our own early drafts by willing all the parts to serve an overall general goal. Louise Glück has written in *Proofs & Theories* that she once valued above all else the "elegant statement" poem; and it is evident that she achieved beautiful work in such poems, which are masterfully transfunctional: the reader feels how mysteriously one functioning part uncannily fits to another. When I read those poems of Glück's, I find myself saying, "Those poems *do* so much!" Glück wrote that she consciously made herself shift in her consideration of the material of such poems; it is implicit that she felt she could only grow as an artist by learning doubt about transfunctional design.

It's my theory that we writers all tend to learn cross-functional design later in our lives. Cross-functionalism refers to an advantageous form *that is also disadvantageous.* A long thumbnail helps in guitar fingerpicking but it makes shoe-tying and eating difficult. A reality-show narcissist politician is wonderfully entertaining, *and* unimaginably dangerous. A gun is a cross-functional form. Glück retrained herself so that her poems could continue to *do* so much and, moment by moment, to *undo* themselves. Her own understanding of John Berryman is revealing in this regard. She wrote that he moved from "commentary to engagement" in the Mr. Bones poems; she wrote that John Berryman never sounded more like himself than when Mr. Bones inhabited his poems. It was disadvantageous for Berryman to allow Mr. Bones to influence the poems; it was advantageous. A bold choice of cross-functionalism.

Needless to say, what is transfunctional one moment is cross-functional the next. Our cellphones are, for instance, blessings, but then are terrible curses. Allowing us to really see what is before us, our trifocals show us the underworld, the world, and the overworld. Well, mine do.

In what passages of your work is the writing almost exclusively transfunctional? Is there something in the passage itself that acknowledges cross-functional form? Will you give the cross-functional its due? If it is true to the material, consider revising, so that the cross-functional and transfunctional elements are in dynamic balance.

When you look at your revised passage, is it perfect? Is it astonishingly imperfect, having both utilitarian form *and* offering what Nabokov termed "nonutilitarian delight"?

Do you picture a reader who wants that particular poem or story to be cross-functional, to offer the cure for the virus *and* the virus? As for me, if your emergency poem removes my gallbladder at the moment my burst appendix will kill me, I'm thankful.

Going anywhere—then: anywhere

Fiction promises to cease as if that is its purpose. Making no promises, refusing to be purposive, poetry surceases; that is, at all moments it begins to cease. When I feel this condition of here-ness in a poem is about to achieve a purpose or make an ending (and in some traditions this condition of here-ness would be called "it-ness," and in others "suchness"), I also feel how the path in and through the poem appears and disappears. Language itself often appears to be a veil of leaves that has fallen over the path. Poetry seems, to some degree, to be translitic; it makes the sound of a foreign language inside the familiar language from which it is composed; it is a "foreign body" that you feel has come from your own body.

The poem, whether or not it has overt narrative direction, abides in the here...here...here... experience, showing the ultimate respect for the unending. Poetry acknowledges the human illusions of direction and the prose reader's delusions of beginning, middle, and end, while it heightens the reader's awareness of accumulated and accumulating wished-for endings that have not and will not come. Shadows move there, so nothing in my orientation to scale stays constant. There are cairns at the river-crossings in a poem, and they are so compelling on their own terms that they ask me to cross and to take pleasure in crossing at the place I will most certainly drown, unendingly drown.

The prose writer writes sentences. The prose writer believes in the sentence. The prose writer is sure that the sentence exists. After all, words put together form patterns of meaning, right? Prose writers believe that we can construct sentences in differing degrees of transportative force, so that the reader can ride them to a shore: the experience of idea, character, theme.

The poet does not write in sentences. The poet believes the sentence exists but is *not sure*. After all, words put together form patterns of music that cause sensory stimuli at the very same time they strip away the ability to limit interpretation of the stimuli. (This inability to interpret stimuli is, by the way, called "agnosia.")

The poet creates poetic lines of differing rhythmic pulses so that the reader can feel the body of a wave and almost drown inside it.

In the sentence, grammar rules and regulates the rhythms of think-sounding.

In the poetic line, syntax frees and makes flexible the rhythms of sound-thinking.

These particular terms come from speech discourse studies. They have been helpful to me in my three decades of studying the human voice. A person is think-sounding when he is following the sound of his thoughts to the next thought. A person is sound-thinking when he is following the sound of his thoughts to the next sound.

Think-sounding is apparent in this kind of shapely utterance: "I had a nightmare that I was a beast. I was in a beast's skin. I was snorting. It woke me up."

Sound-thinking is apparent in this kind of utterance: the first couplet from Thom Gunn's "Moly": "Nightmare of beasthood, snorting, how to wake. / I woke. What beasthood skin she made me take?" We could say that from this sound-thinking a question-sound or a sound-question arose: something about the true self, perhaps; something about transformation; something about Circe, about the shipmates of Odysseus, all of the above.

The prose sentences I wrote—"I had a nightmare that I was a beast. I was in a beast's skin. I was snorting. It woke me up"—*impart* the waking moment as an out-of-the-body experience. Because the sentences suggest a relationship between form and content, we can figure out what has been constructed for us.

The poetic lines Thom Gunn wrote *enact* an experience both out of the body and very much in the body: the experience of waking transformed inside a poem. In poetry, which does *not* insist upon a relationship between form and content, we feel with great force—and with *clarity—in the body of the poem that has interpenetrated our bodies*—what has been created for us.

A sentence constructs a figure that figures.

A poetic line creates a body that embodies.

The think-sounding constructions of sentences make them concrete in form; so they inherently wish to accommodate a certain amount of abstract expression. The sound-thinking creations of poetic lines make them inherently quicksilver in form; so they inherently wish to accommodate a certain amount of concrete expressiveness.

The quicksilver form invites us to feel the "something-there sensation" and it gains its energy through variation. The concrete form dynamically instructs us in complex comprehendings, and it gains its energy through iteration.

The sentence constructs completeness through its iterations of comprehension.

The poetic line creates fullness through its variations of prehension.

No need to be absolute about it: the poetic line, making its own syntax over the ground, will sometimes verge into being a sentence; the sentence, destination-driven, will sometimes verge into being a poetic line.

Here is an example of fiction in which sentence and poetic line appear nested one inside the other. The opening of Herta Muller's stunning short novel, *Nadirs*:

> Purple blossoms next to fences, marigold with its greenish fruit between the children's baby teeth.
>
> Grandfather said that marigold leaves make you stupid, you mustn't eat them. And you don't want to be stupid now, do you?

Do you sense three eight-syllable poetic lines in that one-sentence paragraph? "Purple blossoms next to fences, / marigold with its greenish fruit / between the children's baby teeth"?

What happens to me as I read great prose is that my ways of *becoming* are changed by the destinations I arrive at sentence by sentence. A new destination is proclaimed. At its best, a sentence is a splendid proclaiming thing. And having claimed to represent its subject, the sentence proclaims (claims for) its subject.

What happens to me as I read great poetry is that my ways of *being* are changed by the ground I rhythmically move over, and I agree with Susanne Langer, that no matter its apparent subject, the poem's ground is the poem's own "morphology of feeling." Having claimed to *be* its subject, the poetic line declaims (claims against) its subject.

When I read a great poem, I feel how radically it resists itself: when it teaches something, its own body defies the knowledge offered; when it subverts teaching, its own body insists on learning; at crucial moments, the poem does not so much *shift direction* as it shifts the ground of space-time in the vital broken rhythms of language. Prose fiction, whether it concentrates primarily on interior or exterior dramas, has a sense of moving from here to there.

The sentence pushes. The poetic line moves.

While *moved* can refer to movement in several different directions depending on one's perspective, *pushed* nearly always implies movement in a forward direction.

Really short prose that exists in the middle distance between prose and poetry, what some people call the prose poem, is for me great fruitful ground because in its form, it is already paradoxical: it is a poem, it is a piece of prose, it is both at the same time, and they are in resistance to each other.

Certain works of poetry carry in them the poet's reckoning with the dynamic balance in which the plot is in conflict with the poem. (I find it in James Schuyler's poems, actually all of his poems, but, in particular, his very long poems.) Certain works of fiction carry in them the fiction writer's reckoning with the dynamic balance of the plot in conflict with the poetry. (I find it in Clarice Lispector's work, particularly her novellas.)

The prose writer, at last, constructs sentences that belong more to the writer than to the work. The poet creates poetic lines that belong more to the poem than the poet. The reader knows, for instance, that the author constructed the stable, authentic "I" in fiction and nonfiction. The reader is unsure how that "I" arose in so many varying, authentic manifestations in the poem.

The poetic line breaks the line upon which we might stand. It ends it. I did *not* say it creates a muddied, vague line. It embodies a dynamically confounding body, not a confusing one. The poetic line is the ending-body of an ending-sound: Line *end*. Line, *end*. We begin each poetic line hearing it say the same thing a bell says each time it rings: Sound *end*. Sound, *end*.

Occasional structures

Artists advance in their craft by focusing on the work before us—it's work that we're still working on—it's craft that we're still crafting. The dedicated practice of workmanship gives us, over time, many ways to more and more confidently place our hands on the material before us. The disciplined effort of craftsmanship gives us an array of techniques. In the constant effort of artisan and artist, working and crafting, constructing and creating, we don't fixate on whether we are one or the other because we know we must be both.

With this "constructs" | "creates" dichotomy, I refer to a statement by G.K. Chesterton that rings so true to me. He writes, "The whole difference between construction and creation is this: a thing constructed can only be loved after it is constructed; but a thing created is loved before it exists."

Looking at the body of your work, do you wonder if it will endure? I like the distinction sometimes made in anthropology and art history and archeology between the word *endure* and the word *perdure.* An enduring thing is a familiar thing that has remained familiar to us as time passes; things of its kind continue to be reproduced; it continues valued, cherished conditions of durability. A beautifully crafted riding saddle made in 1850 and still in use; a uniquely designed windmill out in the desert and still drawing water a century later: these are enduring things. The ruins of a ship much more haunting and absorbing to view than the new and recognizable ship ever was; the painting with centuries of grit darkening and in fact obscuring so much of it so deeply that the original can never again be reproduced: these are perduring things. A perduring thing, shaped by different occasions of change, is very obviously not a thing that is durable, while it is very definitely a thing that is lasting.

What you have made *on a certain occasion* is a remarkable thing that on a different occasion will seem trivial, a humble thing that on a different occasion will seem remarkably lasting.

All enduring work and craft is occasional, enduring beauty, meaningfully reproducible.

All perduring work and craft is occasional, perduring beauty, marvelously irreproducible.

One of the reasons for apprenticeship in woodworking and glassblowing and blacksmithing is to have someone provide the little toehold of having the words "tension, compression, torsion, shear, and bending" for the five forces eternally reenacted by such materials as wood, glass, and iron. This is the "force absorption" of the material, the master tells the apprentice—the master who is herself trying to have certain qualities of force absorption—the apprentice who wishes to outstrip the master in the qualities of force absorption.

Needless to say, no good teacher and no good learner make the terms more important than the practice; no one can do for you the work and the craft of giving you intimate firsthand understanding of "force absorption." Does it help to know that term? Does it increase by fivefold your pleasure in the *grain structure* of the material?

The master and the apprentice always end up acknowledging that in the long life of an artist, pleasure helps.

Good strange

I was not looking ahead. I was looking at my feet. And I was about to bump into a tree—when I saw on the ground an oak leaf nearly a foot long. Freaky. Unreal. I brought it to a Warren Wilson College undergraduate student, a truly inspired and inspiring naturalist, and asked her to help me understand. "Why?" I asked. The very next day she brought the thing to my office and said, "Gigantism." We both stared at it with wonder. Something like this is not lovely-beautiful. It is terribly beautiful, awfully beautiful. She explained that in less than perfect conditions, a tree will make leaves with a larger surface in order to maximize the insufficient light reaching them.

"Less than perfect conditions." Good as the motto above the doors at the hospital entrance, at the hospital exit. Good on a tombstone. Good on the signage of the First Holy Church of Literature where the growing writer places faith in their irrational beliefs in the ordered patterns of construction and the chaotic self-creating impulses of making and finding sentences and sentence-silences.

In less than perfect conditions the writer becomes restless with the shining, holy texts, the concordances to the text, the rules for art imposed by the texts. If the writer is both scholar and author they are fine with the word "text," but otherwise that very word smells to them of the pew and the prayer mat and the stentorian self-appointed Minister of Art who, given the choice, will predictably speak at great length at a pulpit in a place called an "Auditorium" or "Performance Space," or "Hall."

Despite it all, writers find a way to transform themselves. Provided with the so-called "perfect" instruments for control and self-control, writers will alter the instruments in order to reach light.

We make ourselves strange. We are made strange. Hard to remember what chose us, what we chose.

What is before us is enough.

What is before us is enough.

(after Bashō)

Bashō is this novelist's favorite novelist, since I would, if I could, revise the three hundred-page drafts of my novels to three lines of such grace in compression. Reading Bashō, I have come to believe that I know utterly his ways of being and of becoming, the shapes of his will, his willingness and his willfulness, the many forms of his narrative sensibility—a term that, as I use it, encloses his morality, his relationship to nature and to humankind, the full scale of his objective and subjective stances, his reactive and responsive manner as a storyteller. Through reading the haiku and rereading them, I have felt myself inhabit Bashō's peculiar stance, which placed him in a middle distance that was the common place from which he could exalt the commonplace.

Bashō was not the man writing the poem, not exactly. Bashō was the name this man Matsuo Kinsaku gave to his sensibility as a poet, the word for the banana tree he transplanted in each place to which he transplanted himself as a writer and teacher. As a writer, I relate to feeling ripped up by the roots in each transition of my writing life; as a teacher, I take seriously the lesson of Bashō as one whose students knew they could never find him in the same place, occupying one unchanging aesthetic. He sought uncertain ground and he invited those who would learn to that ground, and, as if to say that even his self-understanding was uncertain, he gave the sensibility from which he wrote and taught a name that was not his name but that he could inhabit—by writing and teaching.

Bashō understood that we read poetry and fiction not to find a position of understanding in which we are fully aware—but a place of habitation in which we are fully alive.

The Happiness Question

At its best, literature, which is not at all obliged to imitate life, offers life's mostly unaccepted invitation to *look* and, as a result, to focus upon the essential questions of human happiness. It invites the reader to look in such a way that allows them to feel they have entered and gone far inside the healing and wounding questions of what defines happiness and undoes it and deepens it, often all at the same moment.

It would be possible to define "story" as an incidence of singular, multiple, and repetitive happiness observed closely.

The moment of observing and being observed might prove to be questionably pleasurable, enigmatically pleasurable, disturbingly pleasurable, bewilderingly pleasurable. It might be a welcomed and welcoming moment, and an unwelcomed moment, an experience feeling intimate and distant, engaging and estranging. This pleasure-making, pleasure-taking moment of looking can seem too brief but of inappropriate duration, dreamlike and nightmarish. It invites confoundedness and discernment. It is neither clearly comic nor clearly tragic, though it may occur in a larger context of moments that give the illusion of being one or the other.

The Happiness Question has precedence for most of us. The philosopher Robert Nozick makes the case for this in his book, *The Examined Life*, in which he asks whether advertising is designed to appeal to people who seek Happiness above all else, whether propaganda works best on a population that gives Happiness the highest value, whether the pursuit of education, of religion, of government, of friendship, of love, of war, of art is always and is finally in the cause of experiencing happiness—whether or not it produces or ends in unhappiness. He allies himself with Freud's "pleasure principle" and its "subordinate reality principle"; that is, he assumes it is true we seek pleasure and try to avoid pain, that the real world sometimes requires us to give up pleasure but we tend to believe that is only momentarily necessary in order for us to gain later pleasure.

In the language of the stories and poems that most lay claim to us we are fully present to the limitless pleasure-taking and pleasure-making happiness we could not have imagined; coming to terms with that wonder, we are also fully present to the compelling mysteries of our *denial* of pleasure-taking and pleasure-making happiness.

This makes sense if you believe as I do that we tend to keep secret from others our unboundaried pains and to keep *more absolutely* secret from others *and from ourselves* our unboundaried joys.

If we call to mind that famous first sentence of *Anna Karenina*, "Happy families are all alike; every unhappy family is unhappy in its own way," we can ask whether Tolstoy was arguing that the more important question is The Unhappiness Question. But doesn't The Happiness Question have The Unhappiness Question implicit in it?

Yes: it does. Of course, it does.

How happy the world made little Sylvia in Sarah Orne Jewett's story "The White Heron," little Sylvia who was alert to the shadows filling the June evening, attentive to the companion cow's "wariness," and who was able to sense her own loneliness in the company of those sleepy-headed birds and beasts. Jewett was clearly presenting the imminent misfortunes that will arrive with the boy carrying his gun; but at all points in the story, the observations focus upon—give the greatest weight to—Sylvia's will to be happy, to take pleasure and make pleasure, to have not just the sense of delight but the *saturation* of delight, not just the sense of discovering delight but of *inventing* it.

And the ending is a happy ending! Well, it's a happy ending in that Sylvia decides she wishes for happiness on her own terms and not on the hunter's terms. It's an *honest* happy ending—believable, earned—in that it acknowledges the complexity of her choices and, what is more, the outcomes of those choices. The reader's pleasure-taking and pleasure-making has fullness because the passages of observation have invited the reader to look substantively far into—and not just to superficially acknowledge—the possibilities of happiness. We do not have to dismiss the suffering and loneliness of Sylvia to believe that "gifts and graces" will inevitably announce themselves.

Now, when I read a story—any story—that does not acknowledge the question of happiness in its closing moment, I feel it lacks fullness. When I hear a really perceptive reader say how they hate happy endings, with the implication that they hate the absence of unhappiness in them, I always want to say how I hate unhappy endings with the absence of happiness in them.

I blame my obnoxiousness about this on Sarah Orne Jewett.

For writers, Jewett's work offers an opportunity to ask whether we are too restrained in our treatment of the gifts and graces; her work invites writers to revise in such a way that we bring fullness to the work's natural attention to increases and decreases in pleasure-taking and pleasure-making—what Nozick calls the "degrees of happiness and distribution of happiness" upon which human observation most dwells. Her work invites writers to reconsider their habits of drawing a line through the draft passages that reside—at length—in The Happiness Question; Jewettt gives us the opportunity to be rid of the false assumption that too many questions of happiness disrespect the questions of unhappiness, that too much pleasure in our work disregards or distracts from the absence of pleasure.

When someone asks, "How did the writing go today?" I feel that I should be able to answer, "I gave myself pleasure, terrible pleasure, convulsive pleasure, wild and dangerous and prolonged pleasure. I gave myself so much unbearable pleasure I don't ever again want to offer a reader bearable pleasure."

If a writer asks how to undo Writer's Block, I feel it should be fair for me to ask, "Is there no pleasure-taking and pleasure-making inside the work that you inhabit during your processes of composing and that you inhabit more intensely during your processes of revising? Are you defending yourself against your work's most indefensible explorations of happiness?"

Desinence

I have asked myself how to write the story sequence fixed on states of being, not becoming. How to suspend plot but intensify the reader's shared experience with the character. How to recognize the story's shape, its archetype, its unifying elements, without resolving or reducing all.

I have come to understand those to be the wrong questions, and arrived at better questions. In *whom*, in what narrative sensibilities do story sequences develop? In what narrative sensibilities are the stories of *becoming* irrelevant and the stories of *being* exclusively relevant? In what narrative sensibilities is reductiveness impossible and superficial resolution unattainable?

Why do we ask questions that assume we must look *outside* the work for the answers to its mysteries?

Are we certain the so-called workshop story has grown out of the creative writing workshop? Isn't it as likely that such stories have grown out of a literary culture that so fixes our attention on *methodology* that we become blind to *sensibility*?

Isn't it as likely that such stories have grown out of a national political culture in which leaders disguise their real sensibilities with the paint of their agendas, and in which educators accept a corporate model for their place of learning that emphasizes quantity of information over quality of sensibility?

It is a busy world our work comes into, and we too often seem to believe our poems and stories should accommodate that world. It is a world that wants response to be immediate, and we often seem to believe that the coming-to-an-end moment should build a dependable, efficiently constructed bridge to what comes next; that moment, so we too often insist, should not *cause the reader to fall quiet* in the here and now but to stride confidently from here to there, from closing to closure.

We are at a moment of desinence, the coming-to-an-end moment, the last-things moment as our world is calving, sheering off in massive ruined sections: we feel awe in accepting the good and the bad of it as fact, awe in the face of responding to it.

When we are writing our way out of it, it will find its way in. When we are sure we are ready to write our way into it, it has already eluded us. I am referring to our specific era, and in particular to our sense that we can ever—would ever—should ever—write a poem or story insulated from the most recent irrevocable violations of our planet and its animal and human life, the most recent brutalities of torture, war technology, and economic genocide we have bought and paid for, of police forces and prison administrations we have made into standing armies, of military-grade guns we have agreed to put in the hands of madmen for the sake of profit, of vast stockpiles of propaganda used as chlorine gas by our own citizens on our own citizens. When we sit down to write absolutely anything, including anything intentionally nonpolitical, the seed, the seedling, the crown and root of what we make is touched by these poisons—*and* it is touched by the *antidotes* of our particular historical moment.

I believe, as many historians do (for example, Will and Ariel Durant, *The Story of Civilization*) that all civilizations begin with *religion* (humans asking what force beyond us brought us into being), advance to *science* (humans seeking the methods to become the force that carries us beyond our limitations), and arrive at *art* (humans recognizing meanings and methods while also striving to acknowledge the paradoxical mysteries inviting us to be fully alive).

A saunter in the silence that holds the questions

Thoreau had religion. He was good at losing religion. The doctrines of at least a dozen religions (including Buddhism through his reading of the Lotus Sutra) were doctrines that he studied for their paths into learning the habits of presence. Thoreau was a man whose mind neither hurried toward beginnings nor endings. He bided: he remained, he stayed. He abided, which is to say that he accepted the outcomes of biding.

My relationship with Thoreau has been complicated by his journal pages, which so often reference his eclectic reading—but also complicated by Thoreau writing as a "permeable" artist, sometimes in a once-removed persona informed by the Vedas or by the Bible or by something a thrush sang or called, and always complicated by Thoreau obsessively rereading Thoreau, biding and abiding there, sauntering, making the meandering effort to say something about leaving his Self and losing his Self, while making the effort to have no delusions about Self, all on the way to having awareness of his many Selves.

There is disorienting, pleasurable happiness in this manner of losing the illusion of one self.

I believe that if we were to ask Thoreau whether an artist must directly address the issues of her day, must overtly startle us awake as citizens, loudly and assertively make us politically aware, inspire and even incite civil disobedience, especially at this coming-to-an-end moment, Thoreau would pick up his flute, smooth it with his hands, taste the mouthpiece, play something sounding ridiculously, irrepressibly happy and weird, something fear-inspiring and pleasure-making he had heard from owl sounds or dog flatulence, or from dreaming frogs (Journal, 1851, June 13), and he would ask the questioner to walk with him to the place he called The Deep Cut. On the walk, Thoreau would mostly be silent, sensitively silent. He was literate, as far as I can discern, in approximately twelve million forms of silence. Only if his silence formed a mutual field of connection, would he feel anything but the urge to go to his own journal for his own very private singular dialogue *there* with you, *there* with the world, and *there* with the person and the persona of Thoreau.

He might not speak at all. If he spoke, he might ask whether the particular activist-artist's work you have referred to makes you feel fully alive, and he would not ask this in a prejudging manner. He would question whether awareness ever proceeds from anything but aliveness. He would ask whether a person grows from a sun that shines outwardly or a sun that shines inwardly (Journal, 1850, November 16). Between his long silences, he would likely speak—effusively speak—about the iterations of wonder in the natural world. He would offer—meticulously offer—his own subtlest reactions to the observable differences in ground-dwellers and air-dwellers at seasons in which one habit of being appears to end and another appears to begin. He would track his processes of feeling and thought for you and would speculatively track yours.

He was making himself the reader of his own soul where he wished to be attentive, alive, aware. I believe Thoreau made no distinction between matters of attentiveness, aliveness, awareness and matters of conscience. To be fully aware, alive, attentive was to be a fierce conscientious objector to dangerous groups of people with delusions of separateness and superiority.

It is not a bad thing for a writer to saunter in the silence that holds questions vital to storytellers and poets: Is this the beginning of the beginning? Why does this feel like the beginning of the end?

As a steel mill worker and short-order cook and bar manager and night janitor, I heard my workplace friends who knew I wished to be a writer ask me, "What kind of life is that?" I would fall silent, which they assumed was no answer at all, and which I understood was the most honest answer I could give. I think it is Emerson who said, "I like best the silence in the church before the sermon begins."

The long gaze

Part of the joy of writing is remaking who you are as a human being and understanding that the opportunity to undo your life, to enter new uncertainties, is a great blessing. A great gift.

My father, who worked in the steel mill all of his life, wanted to be a lawyer, and he studied the law the way people do who want to be lawyers. He didn't just read here and there about the law. He studied the law. He never had, fully, the privilege of moving past life in the steel mill, but he knew this other language, the language of law, and he was in awe of it. I could look at him and experience what John Berryman called "the stance of wonder."

We live in the world by thinking ahead to what comes next instead of stopping in a stance of wonder and being in that moment.

This is part of the discipline of being a writer—to constantly, every day and well outside of the writing time, in the time that you're just moving through the world—to say, "How will I reside in language differently than I did yesterday? How will I listen differently than I listened yesterday?"

This is why I believe that the life of the artist is inherently a life of pleasure; when I hear people talk about the suffering that is involved in their work, I don't take that for granted, but I don't identify. For me, suffering is part of living fully. Part of being fully alive is pleasurable, but if you are fully alive when you are miserable, you are experiencing something pleasurable. That is paradoxical, and paradox is the very essence of really rich art.

It is pleasurable to experience beauty and be destabilized.

Everything in an artist's life, in general, has to do with the degree to which you perfect your capacity for the long gaze. To practice the long gaze not just when you're writing, but in every waking and, if possible, every dreaming second of your life. To take not just the opportunity, but the responsibility for the long gaze. Because, especially for us in American culture, the temptation is to look at and look past immediately everything that comes before us. Everything that presents itself before us, we glance at. We are already looking for some other value.

Bashō, who was a great poet but also a master teacher, asked anyone he ever taught to learn wabi. Wabi is the spirit of impoverishment in which what is before us can be appreciated on its own terms, in which what is before us is *enough*. You don't have to look past what is before you. You don't have to look around it. You don't have to interrogate it. You can be present to it, and if you will engage in the long gaze, you will already find yourself moving out of yourself into the middle ground that exists between you and that person, or you and that phenomenon in nature, and then so deeply entering it that you are looking at yourself from inside it.

When you actually allow yourself to move beyond just gazing to the long gaze, it starts to kill in you all of the capacity for superficiality that will only do disservice to you as an artist. When I, in my own life, practice it, it murders my capacity for being superficial, for being impatient, and for not taking pleasure and delight in very small things.

This practice, the long gaze, which every one of us can do every waking moment of our lives, is, at the simplest level, the practice of the artist.

Mc McIlvoy's letter to a young writer: the writer's act of faith

In your letter to me you have addressed the challenging pressures you feel as a writer who wishes to be out in the world in order to be fully present to the dark, luminous beauty it offers, and who wishes to be apart from the world in order to be in that monastic lifestyle that Katherine Anne Porter sought, and to be engaged in writing as an art (what you have called an "act of faith") that, in the end, might only offer you "an unloved job and a writing habit that has really come to nothing."

As you have said, the writer is engaged in a pure act of faith that takes courage.

Remember that the writer can leave each solitary writing session feeling more vulnerable and sensitive to her own ways of being and becoming; and that makes the writer's journeys into the world more intense in remarkable ways. Remember that the writer can leave each solitary writing session feeling more connected to the body and soul of every human, animal, and plant; and that makes the writer's journeys into relationship more marvelous.

There is absolutely no doubt that the artist's life is questionable as a "career." I have been short-order cook, nurse's aide, steel mill laborer, janitor, bouncer, bar manager, poorly paid teacher, and poorly paid freelance editor during my forty-five-year questionable "career" as an artist.

In my "*life*"—a far different thing than a "career"—as a storyteller I have experienced a deepening vulnerable heart-sinew-bone-skin-brain connection to humanity (its dark and luminous beauty) that I would not trade for any "career" on this planet.

There is a gift before you, dear writer, and it is your own unique gift. Offer it your all. Be attentive to all that it offers you. It will not bring you more than the world (place of loving, place of being loved) brings you, but it *will* bring more of you to the world.

The overplus: notes from a learner-teacher

The artist should attend to what is left over after each process of revision.

Because of our poor early formal education in writing, most of us were taught to value transactional communication (the argumentative, the illustrative, the instructional, etc.) over transformational communication (the confounding, the riddling, the mysterious). When our instincts would lead us to attempt dynamic balance between the transactional and the transformational, we would be firmly corrected by teachers dutifully teaching to The Test.

The result is that in every act of authoring we too frequently insist all the elements of our work must have use, and we too infrequently welcome the useless but light-bearing passages. We are hardly aware of how habitually we set aside the so-called useless material. We become proud of swiftly dismissing what is left over, the overplus. We picture a reader favoring language's moments of due payment over its moments of vibrant fulfillment, and so, we answer only to that reader's base will to always value the engine over the enigma.

We come to expect all manifestations of dark and luminous beauty to argue for—and not to exceed—their purpose. We consider it a high compliment to a short story if we say, "No single word is wasted," as if good stories were as duty-bound to efficiency as instruction manuals.

We praise a novel's articulate themes and balanced dramas over its thematic paradoxes and dynamically balanced dramas (the dramas falling into and out of balance in the selfsame moment).

We resent how the novella pushes against the outer limits of our attraction to playfulness, to intolerable darkness, to beguiling and dodgy artlessness, to the abyss inhabited by someone unrelatable to us.

We mistake the gifts of the short-short story as skillful distillations of something larger, instead of recognizing them as uniquely expansive mysteries of inverse proportion.

The artist should respect how the reader's desires naturally override the reader's needs.

The scent of the lily's moist stamen, the continued existence of light from passing cars, the imagined taste of the mess on the baby's bib, the sound of the rainwater washing concrete curbs, the skin-sensation of dew on the door-screen: each of us desires to be fully present to these wonders of otherness, to shed all our constructed Selves in order to dwell upon the Other, then to dwell within the Other, to find there an Other Self, and to experience an indwelling that places us at the portal of True Self. Unfortunately, we let life's urgent adult needs carry us hurriedly past such childlike habits of presence: the cherries are what we think we most need; the pits are, so we think, garbage.

If we will fix our gaze upon them, for a spellbinding moment the cherry pits in the bowl are a virus of comets, a koan-clock, a spilled measure of music, a clue left by a lost beloved; in the next moment, we toss them in the garbage if we feel the image's worth cannot be defended according to how it answers a reader's needs.

Dear artists, knowing that we ourselves are so often thought useless, why not wait a moment before disposing of the so-called useless materials we generate? And even when the final draft approaches, why not have one more reckoning with the essence of the weirdly alive inessentials we reluctantly censored from each draft?

When the artist's work looks done, it is time for the artist to gaze into the overplus.

Having painted a birdcage, the artist notices her sketches for the door of the cage. She scrapes the canvas, starts again. Having painted the door of the cage, she notices the sketches she did on paper in order to capture the devil-light on the inside edges of the mouth of the lock. Having scraped the canvas in order to now paint only the mouth of the lock, she allows herself to be distracted by her palette upon which she created the black washes so important to representing that mouth. Having scraped away all of the painting of the lock, having radically committed to presenting only the mouth of darkness and, so, having entered the caging and freeing world within it, she is done.

She is done until she gazes again into the overplus.

Extras

*"There are three rules for writing a novel.
Unfortunately no one knows what they are."
(Somerset Maugham)*

Five Qualities of the Novel
contrasted with
Five Qualities of the Short Story

I offer these notes for the sake of discussion and debate, *not* as an invitation to rule-following.
In joy, Mc

Qualities of the novel

1) *Generative primary dramas* naturally accommodating/entailing secondary, tertiary, and supernumerary dramas.

2) *Expanding (& contracting) narrative gaze(s)* counterintuitively moving inward (and far inward) and outward (and far outward); upending and reversing attention to near-foreground, foreground, near-background, background, and far-background dramas of the past and present; acknowledging many forms of altered consciousness in viewpoint.

3) *World-making* generously inviting reaction (aliveness of thought) and response (somatic aliveness) to depictions and descriptions of space (and time, as it functions differently in each element of setting).

4) *Widely variable story modalities and structures* readily moving

from comic to tragic to absurd to ludic, etc.; readily moving from the real to the dreamlike, etc.; making use of rigid and fluid structures suited to plot-development (ways of becoming) and to perception-development (ways of being).

5) *Theme development emphasizing paradox*, moving through the tensions of discovery/recognition and through the surprises of irony to the dilemmas/crises of paradox.

Contrasting qualities of short fiction

1) Generative primary dramas naturally *limiting* the entailing secondary, tertiary, and supernumerary dramas.

2) *Contracting* (& expanding) narrative gaze(s).

3) World-making, *focused* but generous.

4) *Narrowly variable* story modalities and structures.

5) Theme development *acknowledging and valuing* paradox.

Recommended reading: A *Muse and A Maze* and *Maps of the Imagination*, Peter Turchi; *How Fiction Works*, James Wood; *Lectures on Literature*, Vladimir Nabokov; *Aspects of the Novel*, E.M. Forster; *The Living Novel*, V.S. Pritchett; *The Paris Review Interviews, Vol. 2; Conversations with James Baldwin*, Eds. Fred Stanley, Louis H. Pratt; *13 Ways of Looking at the Novel*, Jane Smiley; *The Hidden Machinery*, Margot Livesey; *Reading Like a Writer*, Francine Prose; *Changing My Mind*, Zadie Smith; *The Source of Self-Regard*, Toni Morrison; *Novel Voices*, Eds. Jennifer Levasseur, Kevin Rabelais; *The Novel: A Biography*, Michael Schmidt; *Art of the Novel*, Milan Kundera.

Attributes of the Novella

The German tradition is root tradition of the short novel. In it, the "disciplined life" (Thomas Mann) leads to:

- An invitation to transcend
- An invitation to be destroyed

Character:

- A novella's main character likely has a self-circumscribing/self-limiting life and has known only one way of life: one cycle of repeating behavior—a circle, small, by choice or no choice at all.
- In a novella with two characters, the second is important not for what they do but for what they show about the first one—a character and a double.
- A novella's characters are as estranging as engaging. They exist in the immured condition (Katherine Ann Porter), the condition of heroic fixity (Willa Cather).
- Whether first, third, omniscient; participant, nonparticipant, POV focuses tightly, solely on a singular character (even if the singular character does not have POV).

Some aspects of form:

- Confined spatially and temporally
- Structurally, no beginning or ending (to the condition). Ends in irresolution

- Voice often idiosyncratic (even sometimes inarticulate)
- Tone: shrill, estranging, uncanny, disturbing
- Extremes of exposition or narrative (some lend themselves to lyric force; may read like a long poem)
- Self-limiting perspective or narrative sensibility. Extremes of objective or subjective view (cold & colder/warm & warmer); this is part of the self-circumscribed condition, person cannot break out of pattern
- Primacy of substructure (repeated images, actions, details) over superstructure (backstory, foreground story, framing story, conventions of genre, of motive, outcomes, milieu)
- Concentration on extended scene
- Extended treatment of setting as character and of atmosphere as drama
- Often includes voids and gaps: erasing silences, comforting silences, punishing silences, white space, perhaps lack of transitions
- The arc of fate is accelerated—a rapidly progressing process of collapse or degeneration
- The testing of reader tolerances (for subject matter; for estranging characters; for elasticity in genre; for idiosyncratic language or story form; for artistic device; for absence of transitions; for the suspended ending

The short novel is a good form for stories that repeat themselves: redundant retellings, with changes, each time, at the particle level, that "change everything."

Voice Collection

Voice Collection Method

Before the interview:

Discuss your motives for the interview: that you wish to collect the person's voice and to study its qualities; that is, its changing intonations, rhythms, stresses, pauses, the subtle and general forces of its music.

Discuss the terms for the interview: that you will need approximately 1 hour to 90 minutes for the interview; that you will not share the recording with anyone unless you have the express permission of the interviewee; that if the interviewee wishes, you will provide them with unedited copies of the recorded interview so that they may give them to family, friends, etc.

The Interview:

Choose a location that is convenient for the interviewee; the interviewee's home is best. Background noise (distant traffic, birds, etc.) does not usually cause problems; other human voices do cause problems; telephones do cause problems.

Do not give the questions to the person in advance of the interview. Do not leave the person alone; if the person wishes to make eye contact, make eye contact; if the person wishes to look at the recorder or elsewhere, make that comfortable. *Be engaged and reactive,* but, as much as possible, do not include your own voice.

At the time of the interview, have the written questions in front of you, but speak each question into the recorder. After the person answers, let there be "air time" for the person to say more before you proceed to the next question.

Test the equipment before beginning in order to be sure clarity, volume, speed, etc. are effective. A good test question: Have you ever had your voice collected before?

Encourage the person to take their time in answering, repeat the question if needed, but explain that you will not prompt them or respond in any way during his/her answer, so that the recording will include as little of the interviewer's voice as possible. If the person does not answer the question, try again, but then simply move on to the next question. Remember that pauses, repetitions, evasions, excursions, self-corrections, etc. are a natural part of expression.

Provide the *permission contract*, but do not insist on receiving it back immediately.

Voice Collection Questions

1. Please name the members of your family of origin (your grandparents, parents, siblings). Give the date and location of your birth.
2. Please name the members of your immediate family (partner, husband, wife, children).
3. Describe your formal education, naming the schools and locations, and, if possible, the dates. Feel free to include the names of teachers and classmates.
4. Describe your informal education, naming the most significant life experiences that have shaped you as a person. Feel

free to include the names of persons, places, and the details of specific circumstances.

5. Tell a little about one of the members of your family of origin or one of the members of your immediate family.

6. Tell a story *not about you* that was or still is repeated frequently or infrequently in your family of origin or in your immediate family.

7. Tell a story *about you* that was or still is repeated frequently or infrequently in your family of origin or your immediate family.

8. Tell a story that is painful to recall. (If this story was told in answer to questions 4-7, feel free to add to it, or tell another painful-to-recollect story.)

9. You may now look at the written questions. Anything you wish to add?

Voice Collection Permission Form

I authorize ________________ to record my voice, and I agree that ____________________ may use the recording in materials related to personal and professional use.

I understand that this agreement may be voided at any time if I make that request in writing.

SIGNATURE: ________________________DATE: ____________

FULL ADDRESS:

____

____

ZIP CODE: ____________________

PHONE NUMBERS:

____________________________, ______________________________

Teaching Philosophy

The whole difference between construction and creation is this:
A thing constructed can only be loved after it is constructed;
But a thing created is loved before it exists.
(G.K. Chesterton, "Preface to *Pickwick Papers*")

In all teaching situations I emphasize the risk-taking processes through which we learn the habits of presence. As in all the arts, literary arts invite us to change every aspect of our lives by being fully present, moment by moment, to the beauty before us. I teach this exciting opportunity to be "radically decentered" (Elaine Scarry) with great passion.

Before I teach methods, I teach concepts that challenge the writer's first assumptions about the will of the work, the will of the writer, and the will of the reader. In teaching concepts of enacting and imparting, of grounded and ungrounded experience, of resistance and receptivity, of somatic aliveness, co-consciousness, and nonutilitarian delight, I invite the writer to come to terms with her/his struggles of willfulness and willingness in composing and revising.

I choose texts and give assignments that empower writers to place trust in prehension (Whitman's term for "the something-there sensation") and not exclusively in comprehension. Having patiently presented a set of concepts framed by the unique circumstances of the course, I introduce methods of composing such as "nesting," in which the fiction writer nests essaying and poetry in their story, in which the essayist welcomes the possibilities of poetry and storytelling into their essay, etc. Whether I am teaching a brief conference workshop or an intensive writer's workout or a semester-long academic course, I am, in all cases, attempting to teach generous, reverent, lucid habits of presence.

Because I wish for writers to unlearn so many hardened assumptions about the reader, in my writing assignments and my manner of critical response I consistently ask the writer to consider how the reader's desires override the reader's needs. I try to liberate writers to be at play inside the work. I guide them in discerning surprising possibilities arising in the various elements of the draft, those expansive moments in which the work presents its own terms of engagement in dynamic opposition to the author's design intentions. In other words, I offer methods for authors creating their work instead of merely constructing it.

Terms of Engagement Between Author and Editor

Good novels are manipulative, intentional, designed—and they are self-liberating. As in life, we readers experience the novel's greatest rewards in witnessing the undoing of our own willful expectations. In great novels, the convergence of the author's will, the will of the work itself, and the will of the reader is a dynamic convergence. In great novels we do not feel balance: the limited stance of certainty. Instead, in every chapter, page, passage, and particle of language, we feel that verging-into-balance and falling-from-balance are occurring at the very same moment: the generous "stance of wonder" (John Berryman).

When the willful author offers static balance in their uses of narrative voice and language, story structure, character development, and viewpoint, scene treatment and presentation of temporal and spatial condition, the editor must insist upon the dynamic balance sought by the self-liberating work. If all elements of the author's manuscript completely resist such dynamic balance, the editor must reject it, asking the author to resubmit it when it is ready.

The editor must not be willful, rejecting work or suggesting changes in it according to personal preference. Each book he edits presents an opportunity for him to dismiss his own and the author's rigid allegiances to received wisdom about "bad" and "good" fiction. In subtle and in quite significant recommendations, the editor must take into account the context of that particular moment and the spirit of the whole. He must be sensitive to the possibilities for natural adherence to convention as well as natural departure from it.

Through full engagement with the body and mind of the author's work, with its individual traits and the habits characteristic of its kind, and with the unique music of its language, the editor assists the author in processes of revision that are, after all, processes of unlearning willfulness, of learning willingness.

Selected Writing Exercises

Five-Sentence Exercise: Transforming Voice

1. **A single "crowded" sentence containing a person, place, and talismanic thing/object.**
   EX.: The long blade of her pocketknife looked lovely underwater.

2. **A single sentence providing the situation.**
   EX.: It was her brother's fourteenth birthday.

3. **A single sentence providing the setting.**
   EX.: Everyone was enjoying the foul-smelling, shallow pool.

4. **A single sentence focused on the talismanic thing/object. (Remember to allow the object to have its own "feelings." That, after all, is what makes it talismanic: It's alive!)**
   EX.: She felt sure the knife, with six unique functions, enjoyed the pool.

***

Reread the first sentence to "rediscover" what the next sentence wishes to be. Reread the second sentence to feel what the next sentence wishes to be, etc.

You are practicing being fully present to *what is*, to *states of being*, instead of what is in the big picture, instead of *states of becoming*.

You are *feeling* your way into rediscovering wonder. You are not *thinking* about how to discover your own intention. You are practicing *willingness*, putting aside *willfulness*. You are writing from the inside-out, not the outside-in.

Don't rewrite as you compose.

Don't worry about transitions as you compose.

The general pleasures we take in what is before us?

Reader's body responding how?

Reader's witness situation?

What kinds of subordinate dramas are before us—

And, in them, what transformative moments?

Fifth sentence—ha!—ah! (felt response, so different than thought: aha!)—the tuning fork passage

5. **Choose one of the four sentences that intuitively feels to you to have many body-exciting energies.**
   EX.: She felt sure the knife, with six unique functions, enjoyed the pool.

   Without THINKING, feel your way to the responding sentence.
   EX.: The sun under, the sky under, the laughter under, the lies, the lies, the lies under the water enjoyed the pool.

Trialogue Writing Exercise

Concepts:

Dialogue in the human comedy: when *nothing happens*

Recollected vs. reported dialogue

The presence of the talismanic object; response, non-response, "attentiveness"

Objective and subjective presentation of attribution; patterns of attribution

The gendered situation; the generational situation; temporal and spatial grounding

The soliloquy: the crowded mind filling the stage of the work

***

Dynamics of three:

One is self-focused, not listening, unaware of the others, unchanging, inward-moving; unresponsive to the talismanic object;

One is globally focused and self-focused, mutable, sometimes inward-moving; comprehensively responsive to the talismanic object but not in dialogue with it

One is self-forgetting, sometimes globally aware, fluidly inward-moving and outward-moving, and is extraordinarily mutable (therefore, a good POV character); prehensively attentive and responsive to the talismanic object (in silent dialogue with it)

***

1. In a first-person recollected narrative, provide the dialogue that occurred between the self-focused and globally focused characters who had an ordinary but talismanic object there with them. The first-person narrator will both recall and report their spoken words. (50-100 words)

2. Continue the dialogue. And now introduce the spoken words of the self-forgetting character (the first-person narrator). Include the narrator's observations of the two other characters, their interactions with each other and with the object. Avoid making something happen. (50-100 words)

3. Continue the trialogue, including the narrator's occasional observations of the object. Avoid making something happen. (50-100 words)

4. Present the single-sentence spoken soliloquy of the globally focused character. (50 words or more)

5. Provide the self-forgetting character's expansive close evocations (prehensive, not comprehensive) of the object: narration, not dialogue. Avoid making something happen. (50 words or more)

Single Sentence Story Exercise—200-250 words

Concepts:

Hieratic vs. Demotic voice; Dramatic vs. Interior mode

Engaging vs. Estranging details

Subordinate and Supernumerary drama; Recent and Distant Recollection

Engine vs. Enigma; Comprehensive vs. Prehensive Experience

Logical (Default mode) vs. Affective structure; Balance vs. Dynamic Balance

Sonic Drama in Silence

***

Narrative Sensibility vs. Authorial Intention

1. In a first-person present-tense interior monologue, a fictional character will present engaging and estranging close observations of one aspect of their own physical appearance and related physical behaviors. (One sentence of 100 or more words.)
2. Revise to make this self-addressing sentence more convincing by giving careful attention to the blend of hieratic and demotic qualities unique to the individual character's voice.
3. Include an estranging secondary story (of 50 or more words) about the physical appearance of one other person the

narrator has observed at another time. (You now have one sentence of 150 or more words.)

4. Now, without providing conclusions or judgments of any kind, the narrator will end by concentrating disproportionate expansive attention on the most enigmatic estranging single detail of their own physical appearance and related physical behaviors. (You now have one sentence of 200 or more words.)

5. Break the single sentence into many sentences and paragraphs according to the affective structure natural to that particular narrator's voice. Include white-space indications of the silences modulating the voice.

6. Provide a title that reflects the narrator's sensibility. Avoid a thematic title.

One-Sentence Writing Exercise—Poem
(with examples)

Techniques:

Individuality vs. Extinction of Personality; Consciousness vs. Co-consciousness

Knowledge (information inviting thought) vs. Wisdom (knowledge inviting feeling)

Receptive, Resistant, Implied Reader; Readers vs. Reader

Writerly vs. Speakerly Text; Interpenetrating Modes (poem inside essay; essay inside story)

***

1. In a first-person plural ("We") postcard addressed to a specific excitable, receptive child (five to seven years old), explain something you felt about a certain place. One sentence of 20 or more words.

   Example: *Dear Thomas, We have a tulip tree growing over a staircase that leads to the library, and we can sit right on the staircase and read there when we want. Sincerely, Bob*

2. Now, revise to make the writerly sentence more speakerly in diction, in syntax, in sensitivity to the heart and mind and senses of the singular reader. Include story (of 10 or more words) about the "We."

   Example: *Dear Thomas, We have a rustling tulip tree bowing over this one staircase that leads to the library, and we can sit right on the cool, rough stairs—some of us prefer the twelfth stair and some the eleventh—and read, read under the sweet-smelling tulip tree—or daydream—or not. Your uncle, Bob*

3. Now, without sacrificing the fundamental knowledge, revise to give disproportionate attention to the essential wisdom. If possible, briefly acknowledge the implied reader in the sentence.

   Example: *Thomas! We have a rustling tree bowing over the best staircase to the library, and who knows why it makes tulip blossoms but it sure does, so we sit under its sweet yellow cups on the hard, cool twelfth stair (girls prefer the eleventh) and read, read, read there or daydream—or not—under the signals in the shadows its smooth hands make, hard to tell the reasons for that, but hard to ask the tulip tree. Your uncle Bob!*

4. Now, in order to be able to sing the sentence, lineate it. Now you have an essay story poem.

Example:

Good Morning, Thomas. I miss you!

Here at school, we have a rustling tree bow-
ing over the best staircase to the library, & who knows why it makes
tulip blossoms
but it sure does, so
we sit under its sweet yellow cups on the twelfth stair
concrete but cool,
(not the eleventh stair which college boys prefer)
(not the tenth probably reserved for college cats) and we
read, read, read
or daydream—
or not—

under the signals in the shadows its smooth hands make,
& it's hard to tell the reasons, & hard to ask the tulip
tree.

Your un-
cle! Bob!

One-Sentence Writing Exercise—Story

Concepts:

Demonstration monologue and Interior monologue; Recent and Distant recollection

Witness, Nonparticipant, Participant narration; Progression and Ingression

Reliable vs. Unreliable narration; Untrustworthy and Naïve narration

Appropriation and Trespass vision; Sincerity of Method and the Historical Moment

Compartmentalizing and Interpenetrating story elements

Stability vs. Instability and Making it Dreamlike; Dramatic and Associative structure

Authorial Efficiency vs. Authorial Generosity; Reader's Need and Reader's Desire

Articulate and Inarticulate Gestural Expression; Initial and Cyclic Phatic Communion

Windowed vs. Windowless room; Temporal and Spatial Suspension—and Imminence

Recognition of the Archetype; Primary, Secondary, Tertiary Drama

Redaction and Free Redaction

***

1. In a demonstration monologue addressed to a resistant familiar listener, a narrator offers meticulous, unreliable

instructions on the task of collecting rain from their roof while they are gone. Write this in the condition of a person who is you and is almost recognizable as you. One sentence of 60 or more words.

2. Now, revise to include the narrator's many untrustworthy responses to the listener's one implicit request for truth about this moment of parting. You now have a sentence of 100 or more words.

3. Now, revise to include a brief secondary story the narrator tells about how they first learned to collect rain on this same roof many years ago. Include specific references to the era in which this incident occurred. You now have a sentence of 150 words or more.

4. Now, revise to include a detailed subset of rain-collecting "instructions" that are utterly useless. Include the narrator's brief essaying about the beneficial view from the roof. You now have a sentence of 175 words or more.

5. Break the story into sentences and paragraphs according to associative structure. As a method of emphasizing imminence, at the end return to the first 5-10 words of this demonstration monologue in three redactions.** You now have a story of 200 or more words.

**Example: *If you knew my name what would you know?*

REDACTION: *What would you know if you knew my name?*

REDACTION: *If you knew my name you would know—what?*

FREE REDACTION: *What you knew you would know.*
If you named what you knew what would you know?
What? My name? My name? What?
Know my name if you would—if you would.
Name, what if you knew my name, what if, what if, what if.

Irresolution in Juxtaposed Unrelated Monologues (approximately 150 words)

1. A first-person narrator will *begin* to describe to another specific but unnamed person a lie they once told that they wish to correct. (10–20 words)

2. A different first-person narrator will *begin* to describe to another specific but unnamed person a lost item they are trying to find. This narrator is completely unrelated to the first narrator. (10–20 words)

3. A different first-person narrator will *begin* to remember only privately a "face in the dark" they saw just before falling to sleep. And now, another "face in the dark." And now, yet another. This narrator is completely unrelated to the first two narrators. (40–50 words)

4. Back to Narrator 2. Continue but do not conclude. (20–30 words)

5. Back to Narrator 1. Continue but do not conclude. (10–20 words)

6. The title of this work must indicate *where* these voices have intersected.

Lecture Ladders

(to be climbed from bottom to top)

Biting Laughter

Biting and biting and biting
Author as wit, butt, and laugher
Horation vs. Juvenalian conflict
The possibilities of reciprocal interference in pharmacies and workshops
Marinations, dilations, reversals
Body laughs at the mind
Where to find a high content of humanity
The disharmonious environment
Carnival mode
& the ampersand
The emotional escape clause
Compounding despair
Comic exposure and malicious intent
The doglike and godlike reader
Lifeless, loveless (bicycleless), soulful, familyless, nameless:
That's funny?
Injuring Chekhov
LaughterTears & TearLaughter
A parking space
Somatic wisdom

God as a Character, god as a Figure in Fiction

God The Loud Bang
God The Colder and Colder Load
God The Swirl of Whiteness, God The Wind in
god "the White Swirl of Obscurity"
God The Developing Character
God The Brownie, God The Startling Cry
God The Exhausted Concept
God The Silent, God The Hidden
God The Bodiless
God The Irrelevant
god of the Frozen Soul, god of the Now-Freezing
Soul, God of The Soul Thawing
god the Church, god the Art, god the Power, god the Money
god of Paul, god of Paulson
god of the "Poetry-spouters"
God of "Is-ness"
god of Brimming, God of Emptying
God The Uppercase, god the Lower
God The Minor, God The Major, God The Holy Vergence
God The Fly, god the Man, God *The Man*, God The Someone
god of the Good Bargain
God of The Ravine, god of Safety, God of Fearful Weather
god of the Household
god of the Artistic, God of The Inartistic
god of Comfort (god the Fur Coat), God of The
Uncomfortable (God The Frayed Jacket)
God of The Mystical Intuition, God of The Moral Instruction
god of Irony, God of Reverent Sincerity
god of "Church Patriotism," god of the "False Elect"
God of The Saved, god of the Waived
God of The Ineffable Incarnate Prehension
God of the Artists, Fanatics, Zealots
god of the Robot, God of The Rhododendron
God of Embodied Engagement, god of Intellectual Engagement
God of The Whirlwind, of The Stillness, God of The Absence
God of The Prayer

The One Reader

"O, Mama, can this really be the end?"
Muller's Ratchet
"The brilliant apparatus evaporates"
"A mistake and the perfection of that mistake"
Delusions of adequacy in the Reader-in-Training reading aloud
Chicago finds Dybek, Holliday finds Armstrong,
Armstrong finds King Oliver
Repletion in the ruins—(What did you expect?)
The gully—the prose cornfield, the poetry wheatfield
The insubstantial, the toy-like, the monument dismantled
"The garrulous meander"
Improvisations, impermanent and ramshackle structures
What does it mean? What does it mean?—Time to pour the cream
The broken poem reassembled as prose, the
broken prose reassembled as poetry
"Direct ordinariness," The Rude Thing—the "tablet
scrawled and nail'd on the tree by the grave"
"You look like a god sitting there. / Why don't you try writing something?"
Aping, writing, aping
Pure and impure impulses
Comic effortlessness, comic slumming, incivility
"A basketball-sized yolk"
Crimes against Mr. Spunkwater and Mr. Sawdust
"A-something, achirp, aflutter"—The risk of writing atrociously
Koan of prose writer: Why wen? Why? And
koan of poet: When wen / —wen?
Koan of prose-poet: When wen, then wen. And
koan of poet-proser: Wen...wen...wen...
The generative wildly, obscenely, radically resistant reader
The Receptive, Resistant, Reflexive Reader
The mental note of C. Dale Young
Unfinished mud! The gutbucket! The unrepaired
drawing! The salvage yard! The wreck!
Let us consider The Fledgling
What the FUG?

"The poet reads it and realizes once again that
it's too good to be thrown away."
"The work holds open the Open of the world."
Readers & The One Reader
The sensitized, re-sensitized, desensitized body of The Swarm
So many damn arms

Lecture sources:

Eliot, T.S. "The Three Voices of Poetry" in *Poetry and Poets*. New York: Noonday Press, 1961.

Martin Heidegger. *Poetry, Language, Thought*. Trans. Albert Hofstadter. New York: Harper & Row, 1971.

Iser, Wolfgang. *The Implied Reader*. Baltimore: The Johns Hopkins University Press, 1974.

Matthews, Sebastian and Plumly, Stanley, eds. *William Matthews, The Poetry Blues*. Ann Arbor: The University of Michigan Press, 2001.

Murray, Albert. *Stomping the Blues*. New York: Vintage Books, 1982.

Ong, Walter. *Interfaces of the Word*. New York: Cornell University Press, 1977.

Shapiro, Alan. *In Praise of the Impure*. Evanston, Illinois: TriQuarterly Books, 1993.

Pleasure-taking, Pleasure-making, Looking and The Happiness Question

The Acrobat.
To play. To "play for mortal stakes" (Robert Frost).
Blindsight.
The dramatic power of the unreal tense.
Acknowledging the nonconscious (the awareness
that is not quite able to become conscious).
The "as if" condition.
Endings, Beginnings, and Life-Indebtedness.
Fullness vs. Completeness.
Boulder sheep, ploughing buoys: the causes of happiness.
The opportunity of "the bridging moment."

"I once met a man who told me that I always had an
exaggerated idea of things. He said, 'Look at me, I am never
excited.' I looked at him and he was not exciting. For once I
did not overappreciate." (Robert Henri, The Art Spirit)
"The establishing observation": orienting, ordering,
controlling, a transacting not a transforming moment.

Cyclical rhythms of life (our-era, our-day); alternating
rhythms of life (my-day, my-hour).
The "best room." A secret broken cup.
Secrets of unboundaried pain; absolute secrets of unboundaried pleasure.
The Companion Within, The Companion Nearby, The Companion Object.
Somatoparaphrenia: the "failure to correctly
identify body parts as one's own."
"...and what-is-this- / that's no-longer-here, what-
is-this-I'm-feeling?" (Stephen Dunn).

Reactive and responsive observation. "A reaction is a small piece of you reacting to a small piece of the situation by selection from a small and preset number of stereotypical actions...In a full response, a large part of you responds to a large part of the situation by selection from a large range of nonstereotyped actions." (Robert Nozick, The Examined Life)

See-er—see-ers—seer.
The plots of co-conscious desire.
"I have an Other-ache." (Roland Barthes, A Lover's Discourse)
Superabundance in outlook and inscape.
Co-consciousness, and the scale of the ardent lover.
Riddles of luck, and The Decision-Making Moment
regarding The Happiness Question.
The terrible, convulsive, wild, dangerous,
prolonged pleasure of the lecturer.
The "degrees of happiness and distribution of
happiness" in The Happy Ending.
Saturation of delight, invention of delight.
Excessive pleasure in Sarah Orne Jewett's "A White Heron."
Freud's "pleasure principle" and the "subordinate reality principle."
The "habitual, good-humored, and therefore idiotic
smile" of Stepan Arkadyevitch Oblonsky.
Perceptual or conceptual viewpoint; monochronic
or polychronic experiences of Happiness.
Story: an incidence of singular, multiple, and
repetitive happiness observed closely.
The pleasure of looking. The Happiness Question.

Suggested reading: Sarah Orne Jewett, *The Country of the Pointed Firs;* Roland Barthes, *A Lover's Discourse*; John Berger, *Ways of Seeing*; Stephen Dunn, *Walking Light*, and *Here and Now: Poems*; Gerald M. Edelman, *Wider Than the Sky: The Phenomenal Gift of Consciousness;* Robert Henri, *The Art Spirit;* Henri Lefebvre, *Rhythmanalysis: Space, Time and Everyday Life*; Robert Nozick, *The Examined Life*; Steve Orlen, *A Thousand Threads* and *The Elephant's Child: New & Selected Poems.*

The Equilibrist & The Dynamist

"Caution. Deep step"
Town love, house and home love, moth-on-the-screendoor
love, dishes love, chicken love, Bible love, blood love, big-tub
love, spot-on-the-wall love, car love. Louise love.
Alligator light, 60-watt bulb light, white piano light,
Motel 6 light, leglight, pool hall light, Vidalia onionlight,
movie-light light, stop-light light, cornlight.

Seeing feelingly in the hither world.
"Outside of a dog, a book is a man's best friend; inside
of a dog, it's too dark to read." (Groucho Marx)
"God is Louise. Louise moves in mysterious ways."
The road trip, The Veals of Deepstep, Icehouse beer, Kurosawa's *Smoke*.
An iridectomy (removal of part of the iris in order to treat glaucoma,
cataract, etc.) and the procedure of odontokeratoprosthesis.

Blur in blur out sensibility and "sensorium" experience.
The *meanwhile* of the continuous present.
The "difficulty" of meeting the work on its own terms.
Dirtied by Wright, polluted by Porter and Cather.
The wolf eliminator and wolf suppressor.
"But I still have some of the pills."
What feels marvelously right-wrong-right here?
A "crab in a square box." An "extremely familiar dialogue upon
which all dramatic writing is founded." (W.C. Williams)
Twitter, Selfie, Selftwittie. "And I remain despairing of the port." *Eke*.

"I have been a keen but unsystematic student of book-length
poems, in substance and design. Length admits them to the
novel's province of inclusivity and digression, but redoubles the
requisite for form. The need for form arises not so much for
containment but for support." (C.D. Wright, *Cooling Time*)
Directionality and Surroundability.
Ethical inversion. The Noah's Ark Structure.
Melody & groove, Groove & melody. "You sang the hell out of it—but
just a little more melody." Honor thy wolf & thy wolf's mother.

Perfect becoming imperfect. Imperfect becoming
perfect. The poem, the white city.
In the metaphor the mind recognizes its mistake. (Anne Carson, Aristotle)
(For more on *expressiveness* and *expression*, refer to Susan
Langer, *Philosophy in a New Key: A Study in the Symbolism of
Reason, Rite, and Art*, Ch. VIII, "On Significance in Music.")

(For more on *five kinds of poetic syntax*, refer to Donald
Davie, *Articulate Energy: An Enquiry into the Syntax of
English Poetry*, Ch. VII, "Varieties of Poetic Syntax.")
Hiding the wolves, hiding from them.
"Every properly proportioned cello has a wolf
tone." (Instrument-maker Chris Dungey)
Quasi-pattern, Quasi-balance. Equilibrium, Dynamic Balance.
"Less than perfect conditions."

Sources: *Dr. Jekyll and Mr. Hyde*, Robert Louis Stevenson; *Deepstep Come Shining, Cooling Time*, and *Steal Away*, C.D. Wright; *Collected Poems*, James Schuyler; *The Making of a Sonnet*, Edward Hirsch and Eavan Boland, eds.; *Messing with the Blues*, James Brown; *The Real Folk Blues*, John Lee Hooker; *Poetry and the Fate of the Senses*, Susan Stewart; *Li: Dynamic Form in Nature*, David Wade.

Song & Call

SONG, & CALL

RHYTHMIC SYNCHRONY, ACOUSTIC RAPPORT
Speaker changes dynamic balance
of centripetal languaging (finding a center) and
centrifugal languaging (forcing outward)

RECYCLING
Relevance of gender-lect and socio-lect
Significance of prior texts—"The real deep
structure of any language event is
an accumulation of remembered prior texts" (A.L. Becker)
Reframing (of context, content)
Rekeying (of tone)
Degrees of sense-making, undoing meaning,
nonsense-making in song and call:
Hopefor-change, hopefor-change, hopeforhopeforchange --------- uh
Howzat-hopeychangeything, workinforya,
foryaforya, workinfor ya? --------- huh?
Howzathopelesschangelessthang, workinferya,
naw-nawnaw nopublicans? --------- eh?

TENSIONS OF AGENCY, TERMS OF ENGAGEMENT
Question of *author*, producer of what is said
Question of *principal*, subject of what is said
Question of *animator*, animator of someone else's
speech—ventriloquation of few, of many

DELICATE OBJECT, SUBJECT
Expressive caution about a charged object or subject

SILENTIAL RELATIONS
Making engaging silences, protesting silences,
erasing silences in the long solo
Aposiopesis (not continuing, rendered speechless)
In dialogue: scale of the expressible (and nested
inside: the inexpressible, unsayable)
In solo: scale of the inexpressible (and nested
inside: the sayable, the expressible)

Song and call of the hawk: "When they are not
screaming, they are mostly silent"

POWER/SOLIDARITY RELATIONS
Dynamics of constative speech (language expressing
what is) and performative (language as action)
Power/Solidarity Paradox—in language, everything
that asserts power over can assert power to
High-Involvement (demanding attention) and
High-Consideration (demanding little)
Instantiation—completing each other's utterances

MULTIPLICITY OF SELF
Kenosis—self-emptying
The educing process of story: what is inside must come out,
is already emerging, of itself will not be held back:
true self behind constructed selves and self

RESPONSE CRIES
Spontaneous expressions of feeling—the long
cry of the wounded ego (Mann),
the long cry of lostness (Gogol), of enslavement (Ivo Andric)
If *authentic* a sense the cry will never finish, will begin new ambiguities
If *inauthentic*—defined by being disambiguous
Pouring and spilling:
What utterances are meant to be contained?
(occasion: task-talk; relation: worker to boss)
What utterances are meant to be spilled? (occasion:
talk therapy; relation: client to therapist)—
story within story (think-sounding) and song within story (sound-thinking)

"Utterances," "Speech Acts"—
"Brette! Brette! Damn, it's good to see you, Brette."

VOCALIZATIONS—SONG & CALL
Song of the common yellowthroat:
SONG (fullness): wee-ter, wee-chertee, wee-chertee,
wee, wee-ter, wee-chertee, wee-chertee, wee...
CALL (completeness): Tchet

Desinence

About finding and being found.
The translitic: a foreign body that you feel has come from your own body.
Fiction, moving from *here* to *there*, ceases.
Poetry, moving from *here* to *here*, honoring the unending, surceases.
Beware The Poetry Cairns
Paradox in the transitive condition: the contradictory ways we are modified
by what/whom we encounter. Paradox in the immanent condition: the
contradictory ways we are always perfecting our own ways of being.

The silent treatment given to the idea of the algorithm novel.
Shape persisting. Shape perishing. Pattern-recognizing,
pattern-disrupting, pattern-obscuring.
Intelligence defined by training our minds to expertly curate.
Incorrigibility awareness (what cannot be set right) and
corrigibility awareness (what can be set right).

Reversal reflected in a modal shift.
Causing the reader regret.
Unveiling *and* veiling, preserving fullness of lostness.
The sensual flooding that makes us feel disinterested in direction;
the cognitive orientation to temporal source vs. the somatic
orientation to temporal echo; the heightened sense of singularity.
Intimacy & the absence of structure hunger.
Dialogue immobilizing the reader, memorably showing people
going nowhere and, so, finding the ground of their relationship.

White-faced hornets
"Afterward I'm amazed at what I've done and feel victorious
without the least confidence I know anything useful or
final about the making of the poem." (Philip Levine)

The sacred void
Beauty: powerful, sensible, and purposeful. Beauty:
power-relenting, insensible, and purposeless.

The nonrepresentable. The representable.
Holiness/horror. Horror/holiness.

The ender. The endling.
Causing the reader to fall silent.
Concentrated Literature Shampoo
"When the dog barks at nothing"—"When the dog barks at something"
The permeable artist
Bide wherever the work has moved past
uncovering to discovering. Abide there.
A hatchet-wearing goat
Attentiveness, aliveness, awareness, matters of conscience: no distinction.
The mind coming alive inside another's mind.
Not surprised, surprised. On reflection, unsurprised.
"The fact is, I am a mystic, a transcendentalist, and
a natural philosopher to boot." (Thoreau)
"As for the sensuality in Whitman's 'Leaves of Grass,' I do not so
much wish that it was not written, as that women and men were so
pure that they could read it without harm." (Journal, 1836, Dec. 2)

Owl sounds, dog flatulence, dreaming frogs
(referred to in Journal, 1851, June 13)
Living with a "clear, perhaps, even with a fiercer
life, because of our quiet." (W.B. Yeats)
The realometer
Desinence, the coming-to-an-end moment.
Imminence, the about-to-be-moment.

Sentencing & Summoning: Reflections on the Sentence and the Poetic Line

A man says, *lilacs against white houses, two sparrows, one streaked, in a Thinning branch,* and can't find his way to a sentence.
(from "Spring Drawing 2," Robert Hass)

The Poet expelled from the Garden
Style: Choices & Crises
Line *end* & Line, *end.* Sound *end* & Sound, *end.*
Ending-body of an ending-sound
The Destination & The Ground
"The morphology of feeling"
Proclaiming & Declaiming
Pushing & Moving
Ego-centered & Time-centered
Blow-*draw*-draw-DRAW-blow
Going anywhere—then: anywhere
"Formal Intuition"
Pedestrian & Train: Ground & Destination
A good suitcase vs. *goosedown on the warm curve of a pail*
Completeness through iterations of comprehension
Fullness through variations of prehension
Abstract expression in the sentence
Concrete expressiveness in the poetic line
Construction & Creation
Figure that figures & Body that embodies
The magic herb *moly*!
Discovered by dog
Poetic Line & the rhythms of sound-thinking
Sentence and the rhythms of think-sounding
A scene in the Cafeteria: The Poetic Line argues with The Sentence
The Tale of The Skater & The Zamboni Driver

Revising Time

Chronosthesia, Future-thinking

Oscillations of Microtemporal & Macrotemporal
Experience, and Waiting Behaviors

Continuity, Succession, Simultaneity

Stable & Unstable Temporal Logic

Intensity of Time, Extensity of Time

Rhythm-oriented, Sequence-oriented, Synchrony-oriented Temporality

Tempo, Temporal Speed

Temporal Duration: Prospective (experienced) &
Retrospective (remembered) Temporal Estimation

Natural Time, Inorganic Time

The Watchful Present, The Instant of Changeless Time

Heterochrony, Transpersonal Temporal Sensitivity

Temporal Categorization: Pre-perceptual, Perceptual, Conceptual

Time-moving Orientation, Ego-moving Orientation

Monochronic & Polychronic Temporal Condition

Nobleman's robe / inside its sleeve / a firefly crawls (Buson)—Immediate existence requires the insertion of the future in the crannies of the present. (Alfred North Whitehead)—I worried. worried. I thought, What will not happen today? (Mc McIlvoy)—Only our concept of Time makes it possible for us to speak of the Day of Judgment by that name; in reality it is a summary court in perpetual session. (Franz Kafka)—In this sense [the dimension of the present moment] our ego lasts three seconds. Everything else is either hope or an embarrassing incident. Usually both. (Miroslav Holub)

Acknowledgments

Kevin McIlvoy's written responses to questions in two published interviews were important sources for his articulation of his concepts and processes. "A Talk with Kevin McIlvoy" appeared in *Willow Springs 88* on January 25, 2021. I'm grateful to Polly Buckingham, editor, and her then-students Joshua Henderson, Alexandra Jackson, Samantha Swain, and Benjamin Van Voorhis for this in-depth interview. I'm deeply grateful as well to Adrienne Perry for "NESTS: An Interview with Kevin McIlvoy," which appeared in *Gulf Coast*, Issue 33.2, Summer/Fall 2021. The language now appearing in "The Writer's Act of Faith" was drawn by Kevin McIlvoy from a 2012 letter to fiction writer Rachele Ryan.

Published essays containing language and concepts appearing in different form in this book include "The Bolted Door: On Writing the Ghost Story" in *Shenandoah* Vol. 71, Spring 2022; "The Editor Comes Clean at Last (A Tale of One Rejection Letter and One Acceptance Letter to Stephen Crane)" in *Bringing the Devil to His Knees: The Craft of Fiction and the Writing Life*, Eds. Charles Baxter and Peter Turchi, 2001; and "The About-to-Be Moment: Imminence in the Grimm Fairy Tales" in *A Kite in the Wind: Fiction Writers on Their Craft*, Eds. Andrea Barrett and Peter Turchi, 2011.

I want to thank the many former students, colleagues, and friends of Mc who supported this project with suggestions and enthusiasm. In particular, I'm grateful to Sebastian Matthews for encouraging me in early discussions about the form this book might take, and to Joe Scapellato for reading an early draft and providing extremely helpful margin comments and insights. I thank my supportive friends and my adult children for their patience with me while my work on this book claimed a large share of my attention. And Mc and I are both indebted to Peg Alford Pursell, publisher at WTAW Press, for always believing in him, his writing, and his teaching; without her dedication and support, this project could not have come to fruition.

Some of Mc's Sources

Sherwood Anderson, "A Death in the Woods"

David Baker, *Meter in English*

David Baker and Ann Townsend, "*The Line/The Form/The Music*," *The Eye of the Poet: Six Views of the Art and Craft of Poetry, David Citino, ed.*

James Baldwin, *Giovanni's Room*

Roland Barthes, *A Lover's Discourse*

Charles Baudelaire "The Essence of Laughter and More Especially of the Comic in Plastic Arts"

Thelma and Corydon Bell, *The Riddle of Time*

Walter Benjamin, *Illuminations*

John Berger, *The Sense of Sight* and *Ways of Seeing*

Henri Bergson, *Laughter: An Essay on the Meaning of the Comic Character*

Wayne C. Booth, *The Rhetoric of Fiction*

André Breton, *Manifesto of Surrealism*

James Brown, *Messing with the Blues*

F. H. Buckley, *The Morality of Laughter*

Italo Calvino, "Introduction," *Italian Folk Tales* and *Six Memos for the Next Millennium*
Hayden Carruth, "The Question of Poetic Form"
Seymour Chatham, *Story and Discourse: Narrative Structures in Fiction and Film*
G. K Chesterton, "Preface to *Pickwick Papers*"

Donald Davie, *Articulate Energy: An Inquiry into the Syntax of English Poetry*
Will and Ariel Durant, *The Story of Civilization*

Gerald M. Edelman, *Wider Than the Sky: The Phenomenal Gift of Consciousness*
Russell Edson, "Portrait of the Writer as a Fat Man: Some Subjective Ideas or Notions on the Care and Feeding of Prose Poems"
T.S. Eliot, "The Three Voices of Poetry"
Ralph Waldo Emerson, *Nature*

Jean Gebser, *The Ever-Present Origin*
Reginald Gibbons, Ed., *The Poet's Work: 29 Poets on the Origins and Practice of Their Art*
Louise Glück, *Proofs & Theories*
Caroline Gordon and Allen Tate, *The House of Fiction*
Jay Griffiths, *A Sideways Look at Time*
Jacob and Wilhelm Grimm, *Grimm's Fairy Tales*. Trans., Elizabeth Dalton
Thom Gunn, "Moly," *Moly*

Donald Hall, Ed., *Claims for Poetry*
Vicki Halper and Diane Douglas, *Choosing Craft*

Claudia Hammond, *Time Warped*
Thich Nhat Hanh, "Interbeing"
Robert Hass, "One Body: Some Notes on Form," *Twentieth Century Pleasures: Prose on Poetry*
Martin Heidegger, *Poetry, Language, Thought* and *Being and Time*
Robert Henri, *The Art Spirit*
Wallace Hildick, *Thirteen Types of Narrative*
Edward Hirsch and Eavan Boland, Eds., *The Making of a Sonnet*
Eva Hoffman, *Time*
Miroslav Holub, "The Dimension of the Present Moment"
John Lee Hooker, *The Real Folk Blues*
Edmund Husserl, *The Cartesian Meditations: An Introduction to Phenomenology*

Tim Ingold, *Making*
Wolfgang Iser, *The Implied Reader*

Sarah Orne Jewett, *The Country of the Pointed Firs* and "The White Heron"

Walter Kerr, *Tragedy and Comedy*
Mary Kinzie, *A Poet's Guide to Poetry*
Janet Koplos and Bruce Metcalf, *Makers: A History of American Studio Craft*
Stanley Kunitz, *Next-to-Last Things: New Poems and Essays* and *A Kind of Order, A Kind of Folly: Essays and Conversations*
Melissa Kwasny, Ed., *Toward the Open Field: Poets on the Art of Poetry*

Susanne Langer, *Feeling and Form* and *Philosophy in a New Key*
Henri Lefebvre, *Rhythmanalysis: Space, Time and Everyday Life*

Denise Levertov, "Some Notes on Organic Form"
Robert Levine, *A Geography of Time*
James Longenbach, *The Art of the Poetic Line*

Sebastian Matthews and Stanley Plumly, Eds., *William Matthews, The Poetry Blues*
Thomas Metzinger, *The Ego Tunnel: The Science of the Mind and the Myth of the Self*
Alberto Moravia, "The Short Story and the Novel"
Herta Muller, *Nadirs*
Albert Murray, *Stomping the Blues*

Vladimir Nabokov, *Lectures on Literature*
Howard Nemerov, "Composition and Fate in the Short Novel"
Anaïs Nin, *The Diary of Anaïs Nin* and *Under a Glass Bell*
Robert Nozick, *The Examined Life*

Flann O'Brien, *The Third Policeman*
Frank O'Connor, "The Lonely Voice"
Walter Ong, *Interfaces of the Word*

Francis Ponge, *Unfinished Ode to Mud*
David Pye, *The Nature and Art of Workmanship*

Joan Richardson, "Music is Thinking, Then, Sound: An Aesthetic Exercise"
Jon E. Roeckelein, *The Concept of Time in Psychology*

Elaine Scarry, *On Beauty and Being Just*
R. Murray Schafer, *The Soundscape*
Mark Schorer, *The World We Imagine: Selected Essays*

James Scully, *Line Break: Poetry as Social Practice*
Alan Shapiro, *In Praise of the Impure: Poetry and the Ethical Imagination*
Ron Silliman, *The New Sentence*
Susan Stewart, *Poetry and the Fate of the Senses*

Deborah Tannen, *Talking Voices: Repetition, Dialogue, and Imagery in Conversational Discourse*
Roger Teichmann, *The Concept of Time*
Pierre Teilhard de Chardin, *The Phenomenon of Man*
Paul Ten Have, *Doing Conversation Analysis: A Practical Guide*
Henry D. Thoreau, *I to Myself: An Annotated Selection from the Journal of Henry D. Thoreau*
Leo Tolstoy, *Master and Man*

Paul Valery, "Poetry and Abstract Thought"
Ellen Bryant Voigt, *The Art of Syntax: Rhythm of Thought, Rhythm of Song*

David Wade, *Li: Dynamic Form in Nature*
Simone Weil, *Waiting for God*
Ann Wennerstrom, *The Music of Everyday Speech: Prosody and Discourse Analysis*
Margaret Wetherell, Stephanie Taylor, and Simeon J. Yates, Eds., *Discourse Theory and Practice*
E. B. White, *Charlotte's Web*
Alfred North Whitehead, *Process and Reality*
Christopher Williams, *Origins of Form*

About Kevin McIlvoy

Kevin McIlvoy published six *novels*: *A Waltz* (Lynx House Press), *The Fifth Station* (Algonquin Books of Chapel Hill; paperback, Collier/Macmillan), *Little Peg* (Atheneum/Macmillan; paperback, Harper Perennial), *Hyssop* (TriQuarterly Books; paperback, Avon), *At the Gate of All Wonder* (Tupelo Press), and *One Kind Favor* (WTAW Press); a short story collection, *The Complete History of New Mexico* (Graywolf Press); two collections of prose poems and short-short fictions, *57 Octaves Below Middle C* (Four Way Books) and *Is It So? Glimpses, Glyphs, & Found Novels* (WTAW Press); and a posthumous collection of poems, *Singing Lessons* (Press 53). His short fiction, short-short stories, poems and prose poems appeared in *Harper's, Southern Review, Ploughshares, Missouri Review, Scoundrel Time, The Collagist, The Cincinnati Review, The Georgia Review, Willow Springs,* and numerous other literary magazines. He received a National Endowment for the Arts Fellowship in fiction. For twenty-seven years he was fiction editor and editor in chief of the national literary magazine, *Puerto del Sol.* He taught at New Mexico State University from 1981 to 2008, retiring as a

Regents Professor of Creative Writing. He taught in the Warren Wilson College MFA Program for Writers from 1987 to 2019 and served as interim director in 2008-2009. He was a fiction faculty member at national conferences, including the Ropewalk Writing Conference (Indiana), the Rising Stars Writing Conference (Arizona State University), the Writers at Work Conference (Utah), and the Bread Loaf Writing Conference (Vermont), and a manuscript consultant for University of Nevada Press, University of Arizona Press, University of New Mexico Press, Indiana State University Press, University of Missouri Press, and other publishers. From 2017–2020 he was a fiction editor for Orison Books. He also served on the board of directors at the Council of Literary Magazines and Presses and the Association of Writers and Writing Programs. He died September 30, 2022.

About Christine Hale

Christine Hale is the author of *A Piece of Sky, A Grain of Rice: A Memoir in Four Meditations* (Apprentice House Press, 2016)—which the *Los Angeles Review of Books* called "a portrait of a consciousness...[that] will bruise you...leave you permanently marked"—and a novel, *Basil's Dream* (Livingston Press, 2009). Her short fiction and creative nonfiction pieces have appeared in numerous journals, including *Arts & Letters, The Sun, Hippocampus*, and *Prime Number*. A fellow of MacDowell, Ucross, Hedgebrook, and the Virginia Center for the Creative Arts, Hale earned her MFA from Warren Wilson College. She also holds an MBA from the University of North Carolina at Chapel Hill, and has worked in investment banking and in business communications as a freelance writer and editor. From 2011–2020, she taught in the Antioch University-Los Angeles Low-Residency MFA Program and the Great Smokies Writing Program in Asheville, NC. She served as a fiction editor of Orison Books from 2017–2020. She was married to Kevin McIlvoy from 2008 until his death in 2022. In addition to her work completing *Willingness*, she has shepherded into publication two other posthumous books for her late husband: *Is It So? Glimpses, Glyphs, & Found Novels* (WTAW Press, 2023) and a collection of poems, *Singing Lessons* (Press 53, 2024). At present, she is writing essays on a Buddhist path through widowhood, including the Pushcart-nominated "His Body" (*The Cincinnati Review*); "Wobble" (*Still*), nominated for Best of the Net; and "Inside   Outside   In-Between" (*Southern Humanities Review*), anthologized in *Best Spiritual Literature 2025.*